SPECIAL SERIES No. 30   15 MARCH 1945

JAPANESE MORTARS
AND GRENADE DISCHARGERS

MILITARY INTELLIGENCE DIVISION
WAR DEPARTMENT   •   WASHINGTON, D. C.

Published by Books Express Publishing
Copyright © Books Express, 2011
ISBN 978-1-780390-80-2

Books Express publications are available from all good retail and online booksellers. For publishing proposals and direct ordering please contact us at: info@books-express.com

SPECIAL SERIES NO. 30　　　　　　　　　15 MARCH 1945

JAPANESE MORTARS

AND GRENADE DISCHARGERS

MILITARY INTELLIGENCE DIVISION

WAR DEPARTMENT　　•　　WASHINGTON, D. C.

United States Government Printing Office • Washington • 1945

MILITARY INTELLIGENCE SPECIAL SERIES
SERVICE NO. 30
WAR DEPARTMENT MID. 461
WASHINGTON 25, D. C.

Notice

1. SPECIAL SERIES is published for the purpose of providing officers with reasonably confirmed information from official and other reliable sources.

2. Reproduction within the military service is encouraged provided that (1) the source is stated, (2) the classification is maintained, and (3) one copy of the publication in which the material is reproduced is forwarded to the Military Intelligence Service, War Department, Washington 25, D.C.

DISTRIBUTION:

AAF(10); AGF(56); ASF(2); T of Opn(5) except CBI, SWPA, & POA (200); Dept(2); Base Comds(2); Island Comds(2); Arm& Sv Bd(2); Def Comd(5); S Div ASF(1); Tech Sv(2) except QMG(65); SvC(2); PC&S(ZI only)(1); Seattle PE(200); Gen Oversea SOS Dep(2); Dep 3, 9(2); Sp Sv Sch(200); USMA(5); ASF UTC(200); AGF RTC(200);

(*Following Distribution to be made in CBI, SWPA, and POA only*)

A(20); CHQ(20); D(20); R 2, 7(5); Bn 2, 6, & 7(3); C 2 & 7(2); T/O & E 3-17(1); 3-25(2); 3-27(1); 5-417(1); 9-7(1); 9-8(1); 9-9(1); 9-12(3); 9-37(1); 9-57(1); 9-65(2); 9-67(1); 9-277T(1); 9-312(3); 9-315(2); 9-318(1); 9-319(1); 9-377(1); 17-11(3); 17-15(2); 17-19(1); 17-25(2); 17-27(1); 17-29(1); 17-45S(2); 17-47S(1); 17-49S(1).

For explanation of symbols, see FM 21–6.

Contents

	Page
CHAPTER I. TACTICS	1
Mortars	1
Siting	1
Infantry Control	3
Small-Unit Tactics	3
Fire Control	5
Grenade-Discharger Tactics	7
Offensive	7
Defensive	11
Mortars in Chemical Warfare	11
CHAPTER II. ORGANIZATION OF JAPANESE MORTAR UNITS	14
CHAPTER III. EQUIPMENT	18
Grenade Dischargers	18
Model 27 (1894) 50-mm Grenade Discharger	18
Model 10 (1921) 50-mm Grenade Discharger	20
Model 89 (1929) 50-mm Grenade Discharger	22
Ammunition	24
Chemical Warfare Use	25
Light Mortars	28
Model 98 (1938) 50-mm Mortar	28
Model 11 (1922) 70-mm Mortar	34
70-mm Barrage Mortar	36
Model 97 (1937) 81-mm Mortar	40
Ammunition	43
Model 99 (1939) 81-mm Mortar	48
Model 3 (1943?) 81-mm Mortar	53
Ammunition	54
Model 94 (1934) 90-mm Mortar	56
Ammunition	61
Model 97 (1937) 90-mm Mortar	63
Medium and Heavy Mortars	65
12-cm Mortar	65
Model 93 (1933) 15-cm Mortar	66
Model 95 (1935) 15-cm Mortar	66
Model 97 (1937) 15-cm Mortar	66
Other Models	69
15-cm Mortar Projectile and Model 93 (1933) Fuze	70
25-cm Artillery Mortar	72

Illustrations

Figure		Page
1.	Japanese Model 11 (1922) 70-mm mortar in pit emplacement............	2
2.	Japanese mortar battery equipped with Model 94 (1934) 90-mm mortars..	4
3.	Left to right: Model 10 (1921) 50-mm grenade discharger; Model 89 (1929) 50-mm grenade discharger; Model 98 (1938) 50-mm mortar; Model 3 (1943?) 81-mm mortar; Model 97 (1937) 81-mm mortar; Model 97 (1937) 90-mm mortar; Model 97 (1937) 15-cm mortar.............	6
4.	Firing Model 89 (1929) 50-mm grenade discharger....................	8
5.	Model 27 (1894) 50-mm grenade discharger..........................	19
6.	Model 27 (1894) 50-mm grenade discharger disassembled.............	19
7.	Model 10 (1921) 50-mm grenade discharger (left); Model 89 (1929) 50-mm grenade discharger (right)................................	20
8.	Model 10 (1921) 50-mm grenade discharger (left); Model 89 (1929) 50-mm grenade discharger (right)................................	21
9.	Tube base and pedestal of Model 89 (1929) 50-mm grenade discharger...	22
10.	Model 89 (1929) 50-mm grenade dischargers	23
11.	Model 91 (1931) HE grenade (left), and Model 89 (1929) 50-mm shell (right)..	25
12.	Model 98 (1938) 50-mm mortar	28
13.	Stick bomb fired from Model 98 (1938) 50-mm mortar................	29
14.	Muzzle clamp of Model 98 (1938) 50-mm mortar.....................	29
15.	Front of base plate of Model 98 (1938) 50-mm mortar..................	30
16.	Top view of tube of Model 98 (1938) 50-mm mortar.....................	31
17.	Left side of Model 11 (1922) 70-mm mortar..........................	34
18.	Elevating screw of Model 11 (1922) 70-mm mortar...................	35
19.	Top view of base plate of Model 11 (1922) 70-mm mortar..............	35
20.	70-mm barrage mortars found on Kiska..............................	36
21.	70-mm barrage mortar...	37
22.	Operation of shell of 70-mm barrage mortar.........................	38
23.	Model 97 (1937) 81-mm mortar....................................	40
24.	U. S. 81-mm mortar M1 (left); Japanese Model 97 (1937) 81-mm mortar (right)..	41
25.	Buttress-type threads on elevating and traversing screws of Model 97 (1937) 81-mm mortar...	41
26.	Sight of Model 97 (1937) 81-mm mortar.............................	42
27.	Model 100 (1940) 81-mm mortar shell..............................	44
28.	Model 99 (1939) 81-mm mortar...................................	48
29.	Model 97 (1937) 81-mm mortar (left); Model 99 (1939) 81-mm mortar (right)..	49
30.	Base cap of Model 99 (1939) 81-mm mortar.........................	49
31.	Top view of tube of Model 99 (1939) 81-mm mortar...................	51
32.	Traversing and elevating screws of Model 99 (1939) 81-mm mortar......	52

Figure		Page
33.	Sight for Model 99 (1939) 81-mm mortar	52
34.	Model 100 (1940) fuze for Model 3 81-mm mortar shell	55
35.	Model 94 (1934) 90-mm mortar	56
36.	Top view of Model 94 (1934) 90-mm mortar	57
37.	Release of U-shaped pin	58
38.	90-mm mortar shell	60
39.	Model 97 (1937) 90-mm mortar with sight mounted	63
40.	Model 97 (1937) 90-mm mortar (left); Model 94 (1934) 90-mm mortar (right)	64
41.	Lower bipod leg and foot of Model 97 (1937) 90-mm mortar	64
42.	Model 97 (1937) 15-cm mortar	67
43.	Steel base plate of the Model 97 (1937) 15-cm mortar	68
44.	Firing-pin assembly of Model 97 (1937) 15-cm mortar	69
45.	15-cm mortar shell and Model 93 (1933) fuze	71
46.	25-cm artillery mortar (spigot) and shell	72

Frontispiece. Japanese crew firing Model 11 (1922) 70-mm mortar.

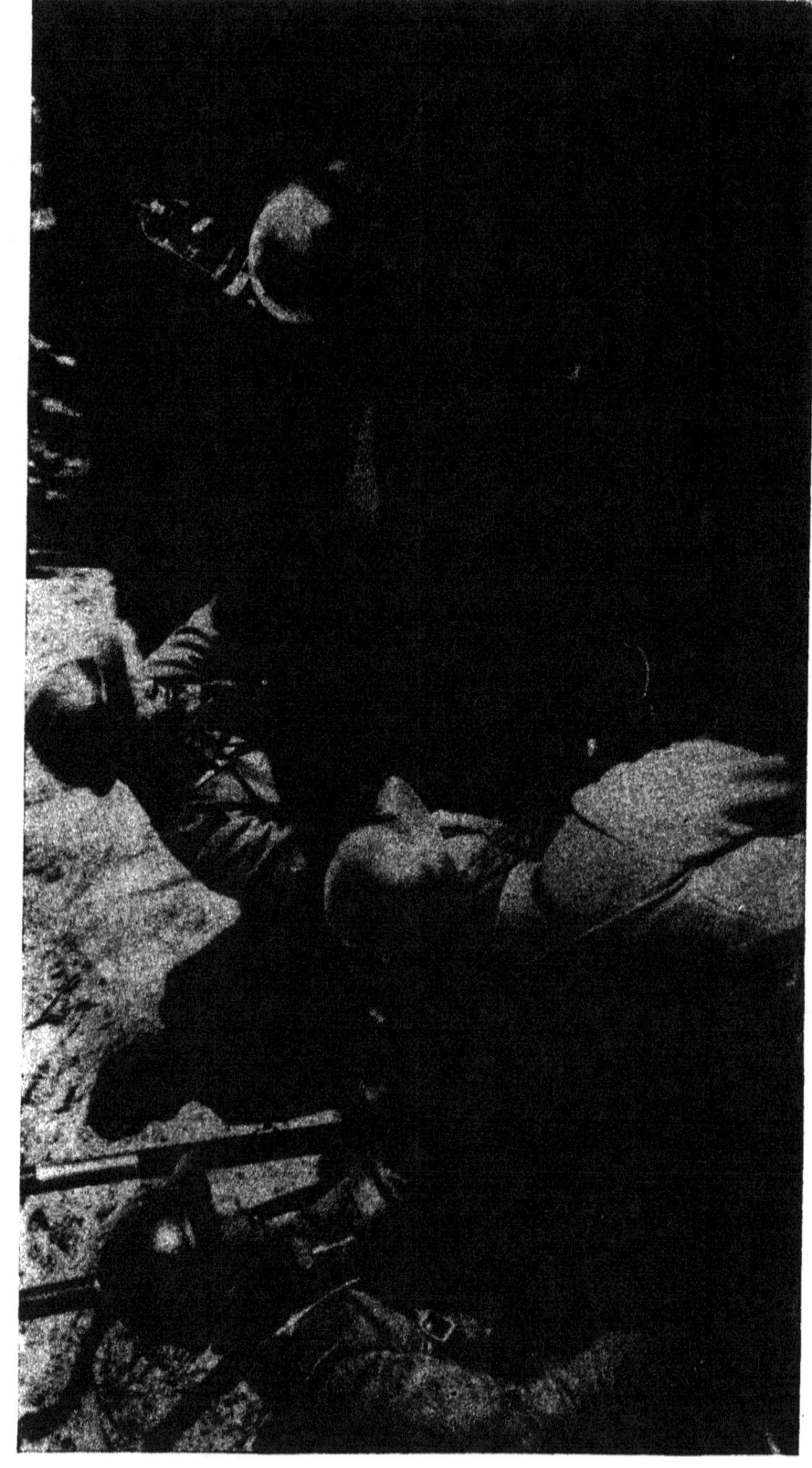

Frontispiece. Japanese crew firing Model 11 (1922) 70-mm mortar.

CHAPTER I. Tactics

Mortars

The Japanese fully realize the capabilities of mortars and have employed them skillfully. The mobility of mortars, and the fire power which these light-weight weapons deliver, admirably adapt them to Japanese tactics which emphasize speed of maneuver and concentration upon the offensive. Mortar units, like artillery, are considered primarily as infantry-support weapons, and are subject to infantry control for close-support missions to an even greater degree than artillery.

There is conclusive evidence of the Japanese tendency to increase their reliance upon mortars. Larger caliber mortars are being substituted for lighter ones, and grenade dischargers for certain missions are being supplemented by mortars. In the Solomons, mortars of 50-mm caliber were employed, while in the Gilberts, 70-mm weapons were utilized. Eighty-one-mm mortars were used extensively in the Marshalls, as they were on Saipan where the hilly terrain was ideal for their tactical exploitation. In the Marianas, where Japanese mortar fire was especially heavy, 90-mm models were encountered also in considerable number. Recent reports from Palau show that, in addition to grenade dischargers and mortars up to 90-mm caliber, the Model 97 150-mm mortar was an important item of Japanese ordnance, and mortars of all types readily were adapted to the cave fighting which developed on Peleliu and Angaur.

Siting

On the offensive, Japanese mortars are sited well forward and assigned the primary mission of neutralizing hostile installations impeding the advance. Mortars and artillery frequently are fired together, not only for the effect of combined fire but also to confuse hostile forces as to the location of the weapons. Targets are engaged which machine guns cannot deal with, and for which artillery is either not available or suitable. Mortars often are deployed together with the heavy machine guns in support of advancing infantry units.

When Japanese mortars are employed defensively, hostile assembly areas and lines of approach constitute the major targets. In Burma, for example, hostile forces came under heavy mortar fire when they reached points 300 to 500 yards from the Japanese forward defense line. There is an extensive use of alternate positions by mortar units in defensive situations.

When a Japanese defensive position has been overrun, heavy mortar fire quickly is brought down upon it at ranges carefully worked out in advance. In some cases, fire on such positions is delivered from mortars placed in deep holes, which are kept covered when the weapons are not in use. From such emplacements the radius of mortar fire, of course, is

Figure 1.—Japanese Model 11 (1922) 70-mm mortar in pit emplacement.

limited; usually the weapon is sited to fire on a predetermined target with the range worked out in advance. Synchronizing mortar fire with hostile artillery concentrations is a favorite trick of the Japanese, designed to deceive hostile infantry into believing that it is being fired on by its own artillery.

Japanese mortars have proved to be formidable weapons in the jungle; even the 90-mm weapon has been used with good effect in difficult jungle terrain. In most instances the Japanese have avoided siting mortars at or near the edge of a jungle or wood. Generally the weapons were placed well back from the edge, even as much as 400 to 600 yards. This practice made it necessary for observation posts to be well forward of the mortar positions.

Infantry Control

Japanese mortar units are allocated by army headquarters to lower echelons and normally come under infantry control. On Guadalcanal, Japanese Army headquarters placed two mortar battalions under the command of an infantry division to which artillery also had been attached, but only the infantry mortar battalion and one company of an artillery mortar battalion arrived in time to take part in the action. The infantry division commander placed two mortar companies under control of an infantry regiment on the left flank, while the other two companies were assigned to a second infantry regiment in the center of the Japanese line. No mortar support was available for the third infantry regiment on the right, and this factor is believed to have been responsible in considerable measure for the failure of the Japanese attack.

Small-Unit Tactics

Component companies of Japanese mortar battalions are assigned tactical missions by the battalion commander, but the details of their execution are prescribed by the company commanders. Platoon leaders are entrusted with the function of fire control and ordinarily maintain liaison with the squads (*hans*) of their respective platoons by the use of runners from each squad.

The Japanese company ordinarily has three platoons, each with four squads. Each squad consists of 10 men who serve one mortar, ordinarily an 81-mm model in an infantry mortar unit or a 90-mm weapon in an artillery mortar unit. Duties of each member of the squad are prescribed, but all members presumably are trained to fill any place. The squad leader, ordinarily a corporal or lance corporal, receives fire control data passed to him from the platoon leader by the runner from his squad. Range and deflection are communicated by him to the crew, together with other pertinent orders of the platoon leader.

The No. 1 man carries and emplaces the base plate. He subsequently

Figure 2.—Japanese mortar battery equipped with Model 94 (1934) 90-mm mortars.

assists No. 6 after the weapon is in firing position. The bipod is set up and adjusted by the No. 2 man of the squad, who lies in front of the bipod and makes such adjustments to it as may be required while firing is in progress. Number 3, who acts as the gunner while firing, carries and attaches the barrel to the bipod. In response to the direct oral orders of the squad leader he loads and fires the weapon from the kneeling position. Sighting is done by No. 4, while No. 5, who carries the sight when the weapon is moved, acts as the squad liaison man with the platoon leader. Number 6 is an ammunition carrier who hands ammunition to the gunner, while Nos. 7, 8, and 9 are ammunition carriers who keep No. 6 supplied. A total of 36 rounds are carried by each squad. Additional rounds are supplied from the battalion ammunition train upon requisition of the platoon leader, who may communicate the request by portable radio. Ammunition usually is sent to the platoon position by pack horses or mules.

Another Japanese squad organization has been described, in which the leader of the squad is No. 1, while No. 2 acts as range finder, and No. 3 as loader and firer. Number 4 examines the shells prior to handing them to No. 3 for loading. The duties of the squad runner are performed by No. 10, while all the remaining members of the squad act as ammunition carriers.

The mortars of a platoon usually are fired as a battery, with the four weapons numbered from right to left. Fire starts with the number one mortar and proceeds to the left. The mortars may be fired in pairs, however, especially at the beginning of a fire mission. One weapon of each pair adjusts on the target, and the firing data then is transferred to the other weapon of each pair. This procedure is utilized to conserve ammunition, always an important consideration with the Japanese whose ammunition expenditure for infantry-support weapons is meager judged by Allied standards.

Fire Control

Japanese mortar platoons usually emplace about 50 yards behind front-line infantry and wherever possible fire from defiladed positions. Every effort is made to find positions which are secure from hostile observation. In any event, Japanese mortars are rarely fired from positions where the gunners themselves can observe the results of their fire. The Japanese therefore prefer to fire from positions where the platoon leader, acting as observer, can place himself on high ground near the mortars.

In aiming the mortars on the initial target, a Japanese platoon leader directs that the weapons be laid on a tree or other readily discernible object. If such an object is not available, the No. 5 man of each squad sets up a stake in line with the target. The mortar is placed about 20 yards from the stake in a line with it and the target. Two machine guns,

Figure 3.—Left to right: Model 10 (1921) 50-mm grenade discharger; Model 89 (1929) 50-mm grenade discharger; Model 98 (1938) 50-mm mortar; Model 3 (1943?) 81-mm mortar; Model 97 (1937) 81-mm mortar; Model 97 (1937) 90-mm mortar; Model 97 (1937) 15-cm mortar.

firing intersecting lines of tracer fire, sometimes are operated in conjunction with the mortars, which then are sited to fire on the intersection of machine-gun fire.

Formal fire orders always are given by the Japanese platoon leader to open fire on the initial target, and this order gives the preliminary range and deflection. It usually takes four or five rounds to adjust on the target; after the necessary corrections of range and deflection have been made, two or three rounds are fired for effect.

The platoon leader, who acts as observer, preferably is located at an observation position off the line from the mortar to the target for safety against short rounds. He trains his binoculars on the target and estimates the range and angle of deflection in mils. Available information indicates that this firing data is communicated to the squads by runners exclusively. Portable radios or telephones apparently are not used by Japanese mortar platoons; nothing is known about their employment of arm and hand signals, although it would seem natural for them to have developed them.

If the first round is considerably over the target, fire is adjusted by "creeping back". Bracketing also is employed by the Japanese. In this process, the range is estimated and a round fired. If this round is either over or short of the target, a second round is fired with the elevation changed sufficiently to insure that it will fall on the side of the target opposite to the first round. The distance of the second burst from the target is sensed, and the difference in range between the two bursts then is halved. The next round is fired at an elevation corresponding to a range half-way between the two bursts. This process is repeated until a burst is placed close enough to the target to justify fire for effect.

Japanese rules state that in firing over their own troops the limits between them and the target must be fixed in accordance with the range, terrain, weather conditions, and the degree of training of the troops. When the average point of hits is moved toward the target, and the wind is in the direction of the hostile force, a separation of five to six times the probable error of range, plus the radius of fragmentation of the mortar shells, is taken as the standard. As an additional precaution, the Japanese state that the initial round should be fired at slightly greater range than the original calculation.

Grenade-Discharger Tactics

Offensive

The fourth squad of a Japanese infantry platoon is a grenade-discharger unit, armed with the Model 89 (1929) 50-mm grenade discharger or a comparable weapon of earlier manufacture. Tactical principles have been evolved which are applicable exclusively to grenade dischargers, but some apply with equal validity to the employment of light and medium mortars.

Figure 4.—Firing Model 89 (1929) 50-mm grenade discharger.

If the Japanese attack plan envisions the use of grenade dischargers in an infantry-support role, the leader of the grenade-discharger squad turns the unit over to the senior gunner and consults with the infantry platoon commander, who acquaints him with the tactical situation and objective of the platoon. A plan for grenade-discharger firing is given to the squad leader; it usually is so devised that at least the first few rounds will be fired in accordance with the platoon leader's directions. Subsequent rounds may be fired at the squad leader's discretion, depending upon the rapidity with which the targets, usually hostile automatic weapons, are neutralized.

After the preliminary consultation between the platoon and squad leaders, the grenade-discharger squad moves to its line of departure. When the attack begins, the grenade-discharger squad advances by bounds in the rear of the assault squads. As the assault squads approach the maximum limit of grenade-discharger range, the squad equipped with this weapon moves closer to the assault units preparatory to deployment.

Japanese dischargers are numbered 1 to 4, counting from right to left. At the command to deploy, the No. 2 discharger is taken as the base deployment. Normally, the front of the Japanese infantry platoon will be divided into four sections, and one discharger will be allotted to each. In a standard deployment, the interval between members of the grenade-discharger squad will be about 12 paces. The four sectors of the platoon front ordinarily will be of equal width, but variations may be necessitated by the terrain, or, more commonly, by the number and dispositions of hostile automatic weapons.

The Japanese grenade-discharger squad usually fires on pre-selected targets at the order of the squad leader. In most cases, targets brought under fire are in the hostile line, and the purpose of the grenade-discharger fire at this stage of the attack is to afford cover for the Japanese rifle squads, enabling them to advance to within about 30 yards of the hostile positions. As the last of a pre-determined number of grenade-discharger rounds is fired, the rifle squads rush the hostile positions. If these are carried, the grenade-discharger squad continues to move forward behind the assault squads, ready to repeat the attack procedure.

When a Japanese grenade-discharger squad is confronted by two targets which must be destroyed simultaneously, or which present unusual fire control problems, it may divide, with two dischargers remaining under the direct control of the squad leader, while the other two come under the senior gunner.

If hostile automatic weapons fire from previously undisclosed positions, Japanese grenade-discharger gunners may fire on their own initiative. The gunner who locates the automatic weapon adjusts his fire upon it and communicates necessary data to other members of the squad, so that a concentration may be brought down on the unexpectedly revealed target. Likewise, if the Japanese squad leader discovers hostile automatic weapons or other important targets not designated in original fire plans, he places himself where he can observe the new target. Firing orders then are given to one gunner, and after his weapon has been accurately adjusted, all dischargers fire upon the target at this range. If the grenade-discharger squad is firing a prearranged concentration in support of the advance of rifle units, however, no deviation from it is permitted by Japanese tactical doctrine, no matter what important targets may be disclosed after the attack begins.

When firing starts, the No. 1 man of a Japanese discharger crew takes a position to the front and left of the gunner, and, at the latter's command, loads the discharger and prepares the next round. The No. 2 member of the crew remains just behind the gunner, a little to one side, from which position he moves forward to replace No. 1 as soon as the latter has expended his ammunition. When all of No. 2's grenades are fired, the gunner, No. 3, expends his. If hostile fire is especially heavy, the procedure may be varied by having No. 1 lie by the side of the gunner in order to lay the grenades within easy reach of the latter, who loads the weapon himself.

Both the Model 89 and the Model 10 grenade dischargers are fired by the Japanese from the prone or kneeling position. When fired from the prone position, the discharger is grasped by the barrel with the left hand. It is held at a 45-degree angle, with the base plate so fixed that the fist is in line above it when the right forearm is laid parallel to the axis of the barrel. The right forearm rests on the ground. The angle of the operator's body is in line with the left forearm, making an angle of about 10 degrees with the discharger barrel.

In the kneeling position, the method of holding the discharger is essentially the same as in the prone. The left leg is on the ground, with the base plate of the discharger held at the center of the left foot. The left upper arm is steadied against the inside of the left knee. In both prone and kneeling positions, slight depressions in the ground are used whenever possible to prevent slipping, and if the ground surface is soft the discharger is moved slightly after each round.

Low-angle firing of grenade dischargers is resorted to by the Japanese "to demoralize and subdue the enemy, to give confidence in checking his assaults and counterattacks, and to press home attacks on his flanks". Aside from this typically bombastic language of Japanese manuals, there is concrete evidence of successful utilization of low-angle firing in the jungle. When the low-angle firing is done with the Model 89 discharger, direct laying is employed at a range of from 50 to 100 yards, and deflection angles are disregarded. Where there are small trees, the discharger is fired at an elevation of about 15 degrees, with the minimum range scale of 12 meters. Recoil of the discharger allegedly is slight at this elevation.

Model 91 grenades, equipped with 7-second delay fuzes, are fired on low-angle targets. With a fuze of this type, the grenade will not be detonated by contact with treetops, and the maximum ordinate of trajectory is about 2 yards at a 15-degree elevation and 1 yard at 10 degrees.

Defensive

The Japanese strongly deprecate defensive operations, which, they maintain, should be resorted to only as a temporary expedient until such time as resumption of the offensive is feasible. Counterattacks are launched eagerly, and, in many cases, without adequate preparation and coordination. In addition to these basic doctrines, the Japanese believe that the use of grenade dischargers for defensive purposes is subject to inescapable technical limitations. Nevertheless, the utility of dischargers in some defensive situations is recognized.

As is the case in offensive operations, Japanese grenade-discharger squads take positions behind rifle squads. The squad leader selects the position, preferably in a defilade which commands a good field of fire and enables him to maintain liaison with adjacent discharger squads.

Small emplacements often are prepared for grenade dischargers if time is available. Otherwise every effort is made to prepare mounts, or rests, for the dischargers; these consist of horizontal logs, supported by smaller logs driven vertically into the ground. The horizontal logs support the barrels. Other logs are embedded in the ground as rests for the base plates.

In a defensive situation considerable care is taken by the Japanese to register discharger fire in advance. Fire is adjusted on terrain features likely to present targets during the hostile attack, and the ranges to these are marked on the discharger range scales by pieces of wire or string. Aiming stakes are utilized to calculate deflections, and notches are cut in the horizontal logs of the discharger supports to mark the proper barrel positions from which to lay fire on the selected target areas. This preliminary registration also is useful in the event night firing becomes necessary with consequent difficulties of observation.

The Japanese grenade-discharger squad on the defense fires a little ahead of the hostile attacking forces which thus will have to move into this fire in order to advance. Three-round barrages are fired from the dischargers, after which the range is shortened and another three-round barrage fired. This process is repeated until either the hostile attack is stopped or the Japanese defensive line is overrun, forcing retirement of the grenade-discharger squad to another predetermined position. If such withdrawal of the Japanese grenade-discharger squad is necessary, one crew and its weapon are withdrawn at a time. When all have reached the new defensive positions, battery firing is resumed. All members of the squad except the gunners may be called upon to act as riflemen if defensive exigencies make this desirable.

Mortars in Chemical Warfare

The Japanese consider the mortar an important chemical-warfare weapon, in addition to its primary role in infantry support. In gas warfare and in the production of smoke screens on a large scale, mortars are the principal Japanese offensive weapon, while grenades and candles are used in small-scale encounters.

At least one, and perhaps several mortar battalions are included in the Japanese Field Gas Unit, which is attached to a field army. The weapons used are presumably the 90-mm mortars for which chemical ammunition is known to exist. It is possible that gas shells may be fired from the 50-mm, 70-mm, and 81-mm mortars, also, but evidence is not conclusive.

Mortar units have been added to the Combined Mechanized Chemical Warfare Force, a new Japanese organization specially designed for tropical operations. This "swift striking force", which originally comprised two or three infantry battalions, one artillery battalion, two or three tank companies, and one or two engineer companies, now includes a mortar unit of at least one company (12 mortars). This new organization is intended to create an offensive chemical force equipped and trained to exploit quickly any breakthrough accomplished by chemical warfare. The mortar unit is equipped either to neutralize a single point by gas warfare, or to attain the desired gas effect on a large scale by commitment of the entire unit. When gas is not used, the mortars can be employed promptly for other missions.

In conformity with the Japanese emphasis on infantry fighting and their use of mortars and artillery for close-support roles, mortars are employed to fire gas shells in support of assaulting infantry. Chemical mortar units may be assigned to a detachment on a flanking mission, or used locally to reduce key points of hostile positions.

The Japanese believe that the purpose of gas fire is to secure surprise, a breakthrough, and a quick overwhelming victory. Surprise firing of red (gas) mortar shells, for even a short time, is considered an effective method of confusing a hostile force at least momentarily, thus enabling the Japanese attackers to achieve a breakthrough in one thrust. While HE shells take a comparatively long time to destroy a well prepared and concealed position, the Japanese believe that gas shells are able to neutralize it in a short time.

Japanese doctrine holds, however, that gas fire is effective only when gas shells are concentrated and used in profusion, and that therefore it is important that the mortar units be committed as a whole when used to support a large infantry assault. The Japanese mortar company uses all of its 12 mortars, and the battalion is employed in a unified action. Even two battalions may be utilized for the attainment of a single important objective.

Daybreak is the best time to use gas, but twilight is also suitable; the wind should have a velocity under 11 miles per hour and should be blowing in the direction of the opposing forces, the Japanese believe.

When mortar gas fire is used in coordination with infantry and artillery, shells are aimed about 200 yards from the front line, according to Japanese principles. This may allow a minimum distance, with a following wind, to prevent casualties to friendly forces from shell fragments, but it also may be designed to allow gas trails to unite by the time they reach hostile positions and thus prevent ungassed gaps in the enemy lines.

Japanese tactics also envision utilization of "special smoke" (gas) after HE fire has been laid down. The advantages of this coordination are that HE forces opposing troops to take cover in trenches or foxholes, and the gas then can serve as a screen for Japanese troops who don their masks and advance as soon as the firing is complete.

Gas is believed by the Japanese to be very effective in areas covered with vegetation and in jungles, and the peculiar features of jungle terrain are taken into account in gas tactics.

The Japanese 90-mm mortar is considered adequate for putting up a Japanese smoke screen on an extended front, with other smoke weapons providing local or temporary screens. Since by firing mortar shells a fairly wide area can be screened, smoke can be used effectively to cover maneuvering, charging, landing, and river-crossing operations without being affected materially by the wind direction.

When weather conditions are favorable, the front which a mortar company (12 mortars) can cover with smoke is about 800 yards if the line of fire is parallel with the wind direction. When the wind is at right angles to the line of fire, a front of approximately 1,500 yards can be covered. For the purpose of maintaining the smoke screen, one shell normally is fired every two to five minutes in the first case, while one shell per minute is fired in the second case. Four mortars are fired in order to lay a longitudinal smoke screen of about 2,000 yards, and one shell a minute is fired to maintain the screen.

Chapter II. Organization of Japanese Mortar Units

There are three types of Japanese Independent Mortar Units: Mortar Units (*Hakugeki tai*), Medium Mortar Units (*Chu hakugeki tai*), and Artillery Mortar Units (*Kyuho tai*). In addition to these independent units, mortars are included in the armament of many Japanese infantry regiments.

The battalion is the normal organization for all independent mortar units; however, Independent Mortar Regiments and Independent Artillery Mortar Regiments have been identified but not encountered. It is possible that the regiment is an administrative or training unit, which, when used in a tactical role, probably would consist of two battalions.

The Independent Mortar Battalion is armed with thirty-six 90-mm mortars and has a strength of 824 officers and enlisted men. The Medium Mortar Battalion has a total armament of twelve 150-mm artillery mortars, and a complement of 26 officers and 565 enlisted men. The Independent Artillery Mortar Battalion has a strength of 642 officers and enlisted men, and is armed with sixteen 25-cm artillery mortars. (See charts pp. 15-16.)

A variant Independent Mortar Battalion recently encountered was organized into two companies. Each company, in addition to a command platoon and ammunition train, had a mortar unit which was subdivided into two platoons. Each of the platoons was subdivided into four squads, and each squad was equipped with one mortar. Total strength of the battalion was reported as 660 officers and enlisted men.

The Japanese Infantry Regiment may include mortars in its armament either in the Battalion Gun Unit or in additional mortar companies or platoons. The battalion gun platoon may be armed completely with four 81-mm or 90-mm mortars, or its armament may be a combination of two mortars and one 70-mm battalion gun. Mortar companies within the infantry regiment are armed with twelve 81-mm mortars, and have a total strength of approximately 160 officers and enlisted men. Mortar platoons armed with two to four 81-mm mortars may be included in the composition of rifle companies or battalions.

INDEPENDENT MORTAR BATTALION

Organization→	Battalion Hqs	Company	Ammunition train	Bn total Hqs 3 Cos Am train
Strength				
Commissioned	(12)	(5)	(1)	(28)
Enlisted	103	197	102	796
Total	115	202	103	824
Weapons and Equipment				
Rifle	....	....	....	108
Carbine	53	44	49	234
LMG	....	1	....	3
90-mm Mortar	....	12	....	36
Truck	23	20	22	105

NOTE.—Figures in parenthesis are estimates.

INDEPENDENT MEDIUM MORTAR BATTALION

Organization→	Battalion Hqs	Company	Ammunition train	Bn total Hqs 3 Cos Am train
Strength				
Commissioned	(10)	(5)	(1)	(26)
Enlisted	119	135	41	565
Total	129	140	42	591
Weapons and Equipment				
Rifle	....	....	....	150
Carbine	2	....	31	33
150-mm Arty Mortar	....	4	....	12
Truck	....	....	15	15
Cart, horse-drawn	30	54	....	192

NOTE.—Figures in parenthesis are estimates.

INDEPENDENT ARTILLERY MORTAR BATTALION

Organization →	Battalion Hqs	Company	Ammunition train	Bn total Hqs 2 Cos Am train
Strength				
Commissioned................	(6)	(5)	(1)	(17)
Enlisted.....................	27	289	20	625
Total..................	33	294	21	642
Weapons and Equipment				
Rifle........................				190
Carbine.....................	6		10	16
25-cm Mortar (Spigot, 320-mm shell).....................		8		16
Truck.......................	2		4	6

NOTE.—Figures in parenthesis are estimates.

A "Temporary Mortar Company" recently has been identified; its organization apparently reflects the growing importance the Japanese attach to the use of the 150-mm mortar. The company consists of a command platoon, three mortar platoons, and an ammunition section. Each platoon is divided into four squads, each of which is equipped with one 150-mm mortar. The total reported strength of the company is 81 officers and enlisted men.

Mortar units of various types are important components of Japanese Independent Mixed Brigades. Three such brigades recently identified each had two mortar companies. Three others, on the other hand, each had one mortar battery and one artillery company equipped with 75-mm mountain guns. The mortar companies were equipped with 12 mortars, probably either the Model 94 (1934) or Model 97 (1937) 90-mm weapons, although it is possible that the 150-mm mortar also was used.

Special Navy Landing Parties, the missions of which now have become basically defensive, include mortar platoons according to recently received information. Such a platoon is reported to have a total strength of 76 men and presumably is armed with four 90-mm mortars.

There is also inconclusive evidence that new Independent Mortar Battalions have been organized and armed with the 25-cm artillery (spigot) mortar which has been encountered operationally. Such battalions allegedly are organized into two companies, each of which has two mortar platoons, two ammunition platoons, and an observation and communications platoon. Each mortar platoon is organized into two batteries, each of which is equipped with a 25-cm artillery (spigot) mortar. In addition to the eight mortars actually in use, eight more are carried by the ammunition platoons as reserve.

The battalion, it is reported, normally is attached to an infantry regiment, within which the mortar companies may be separated and attached to individual infantry battalions. Platoons of a company, however, are not separated.

CHAPTER III. Equipment

Grenade Dischargers

Grenade dischargers are very important weapons in Japanese infantry units and have been employed with considerable effectiveness in operations to date. The main advantage of these weapons, the Japanese believe, is that they afford fire power at ranges intermediate between those of mortars and hand grenades. They are admirably adapted for the close-support roles emphasized in Japanese tactics, and afford a protective cover for the advance of infantry assault units when they reach a point too close to the hostile line to be covered by artillery or mortar fire. Grenade dischargers furnish fire power that is proportionately heavy in relation to the light weight and mobility of these weapons, and the skill of a trained crew compensates for the limitations on precision fire control of the weapon.

Model 27 (1894) 50-mm Grenade Discharger

The first Japanese-manufactured grenade discharger probably was the so-called Model 27. This old weapon still is in use by the Japanese Army, for a specimen was captured during the operations around Myitkyina.

Construction of the discharger is very simple. Its tube has a smooth bore, with a diameter of 1.96 inches for a distance of $8^{11}/_{16}$ inches. Then the tube tapers to a diameter of $1^{7}/_{16}$ inches for a depth of $1^{1}/_{16}$ inch. This part of the tube, with the smaller diameter, is the gas chamber. From the bottom of the gas chamber the tube tapers to a half-inch hole which houses the firing-pin assembly. There is a $1/_2$-inch gas port in the side of the tube over which fits a two-hole gas regulator cap.

The base of the tube is bored and threaded to receive the pedestal. There is a hole in the threaded end of the pedestal, and a groove cut in the side of the pedestal has its lower end flush with the base of the hole. This groove receives the trigger assembly.

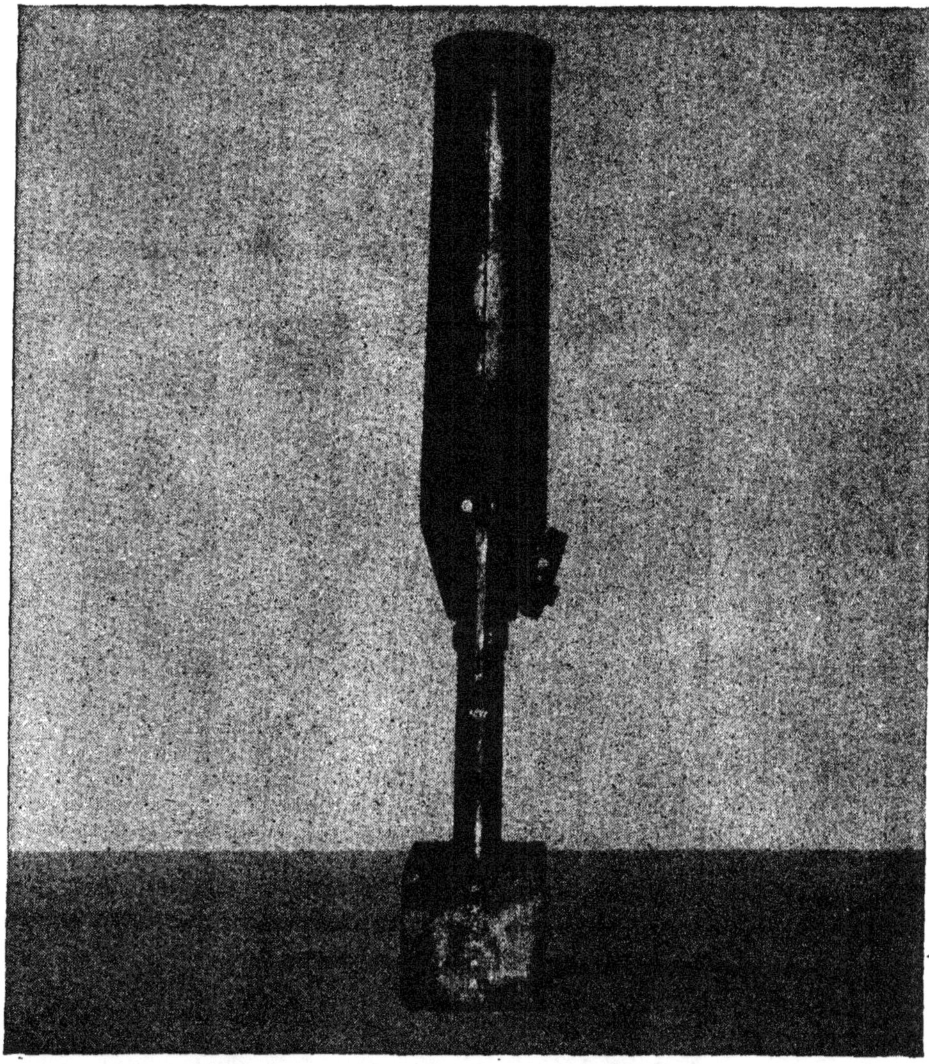

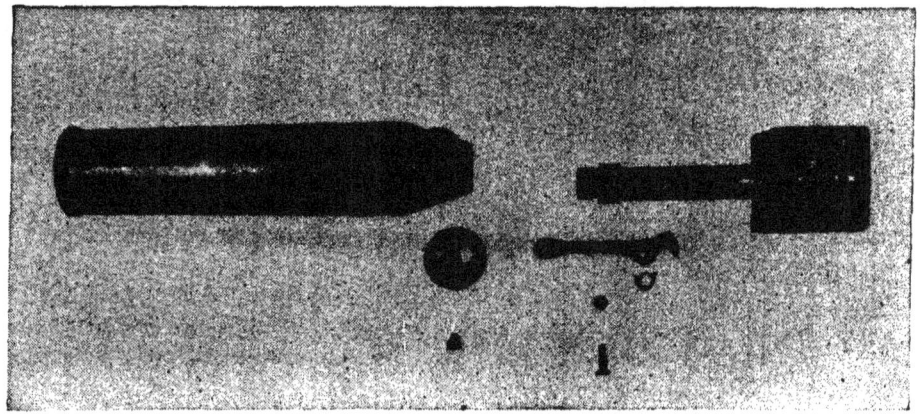

Figure 5.—*Model 27 (1894) 50-mm grenade discharger. Note gas regulator cap on lower right side of tube.*

Figure 6.—*Model 27 (1894) 50-mm grenade discharger disassembled. Note gas port on tube, gas port cap, and trigger assembly. Pedestal screws into internally threaded base of tube.*

Model 10 (1921) 50-mm Grenade Discharger

Both the Model 10 (1921) and the Model 89 (1929) 50-mm grenade dischargers are widely used by Japanese infantry. The older weapon, commonly known as the "10 Year Model", now is chiefly employed to fire pyrotechnic signals, but it also can fire the Model 91 (1931) grenade.

The Model 10 is distinguished from the Model 89 by its smooth bore and the use of a gas port in the barrel to regulate range. It is fired by a firing pin operated by a lever on the outside of the discharger body. When firing, it is attached to a small concave base plate which is used as a spade.

Specifications:
```
Over-all length..............................................20 inches.
Length of barrel.............................................9½ inches.
Complete weight..............................................5½ pounds.
Range with Model 91 (1931) HE grenade....................65-175 yards.
```

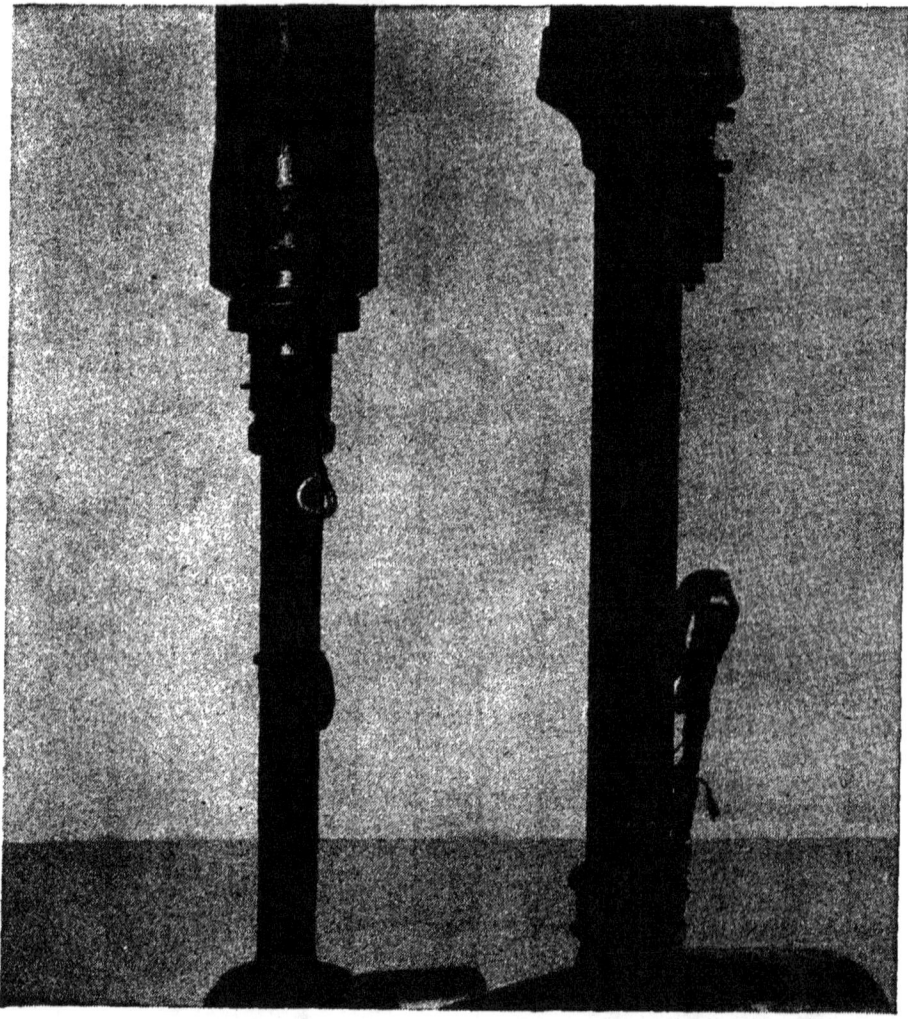

Figure 7.—Model 10 (1921) 50-mm grenade discharger (left); Model 89 (1929) 50-mm grenade discharger (right). Note gas port in tube base of Model 10 and elevating knob on Model 89. Compare firing lever of Model 10 with trigger and lanyard of Model 89.

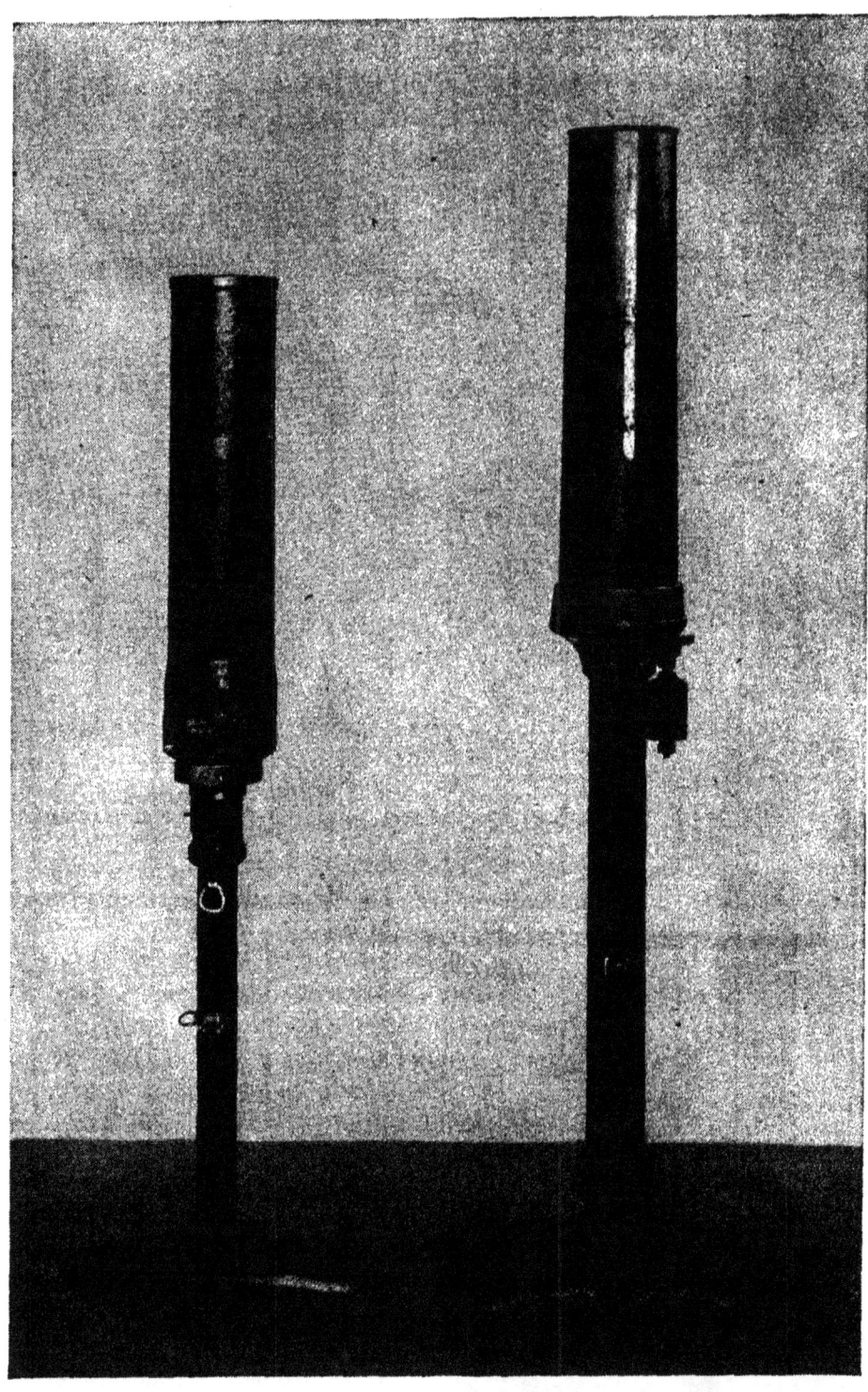

Figure 8.—Model 10 (1921) 50-mm grenade discharger (left); Model 89 (1929) 50-mm grenade discharger (right). Model 10 is 4 inches shorter than Model 89; tube of Model 10 is ½ inch shorter than that of Model 89. Note difference in base plates of two weapons.

Model 89 (1929) 50-mm Grenade Discharger

The Model 89 (1929) 50-mm grenade discharger is a rifled weapon. Gas expansion in the tube presses the rotating band of the projectile against the rifling of the tube, causing rotation of the shell to ensure greater range and accuracy of fire than is possible with the smooth-bored Model 10.

The Model 89 has a barrel, 10 inches long, attached to a small concave base plate. This concave shape of the base plate was responsible for the wholly erroneous belief that the weapon was intended to be fired with the plate held against the knee or thigh of the operator, and serious injuries resulted to Allied personnel who attempted to fire it in this fashion. The term "knee mortar" as applied to the piece is completely misleading, for the plate is used as a spade or is rested on a log or other suitable object.

The trigger housing is on the pedestal, and the firing-pin housing which moves up and down in the barrel is adjustable. The trigger protrudes through the slot of the trigger housing and cocks and fires the piece in one operation. A range-adjusting assembly is attached to the base cap of the barrel. The scale for firing the Model 89 (1929) HE shell is on the left of the tube and is adjusted from 120 to 650 meters (131.2 to 710.8 yards). On the right of the tube is the scale for firing the Model 91 (1931) grenade, graduated from 40 to 190 meters (43.7 to 207.8 yards). The desired range for each projectile is set by turning the elevating knob of the proper range scale which lengthens or shortens the firing-pin housing extending inside the barrel. Thus the volume of the gas chamber can be varied, to govern range.

Specifications of the discharger are:

Over-all length...24 inches.
Length of barrel..10 inches.
Weight.........10¼ pounds.
Weight of Model 89
(1929) HE shell..1 pound, 12 ounces.
Weight of Model 91
(1931) grenade...1 pound, 2.8 ounces (with propellant).

Figure 9.—Tube base and pedestal of Model 89 (1929) 50-mm grenade discharger. Range scale is on left. Elevating knob adjusts length of firing-pin housing extending inside tube.

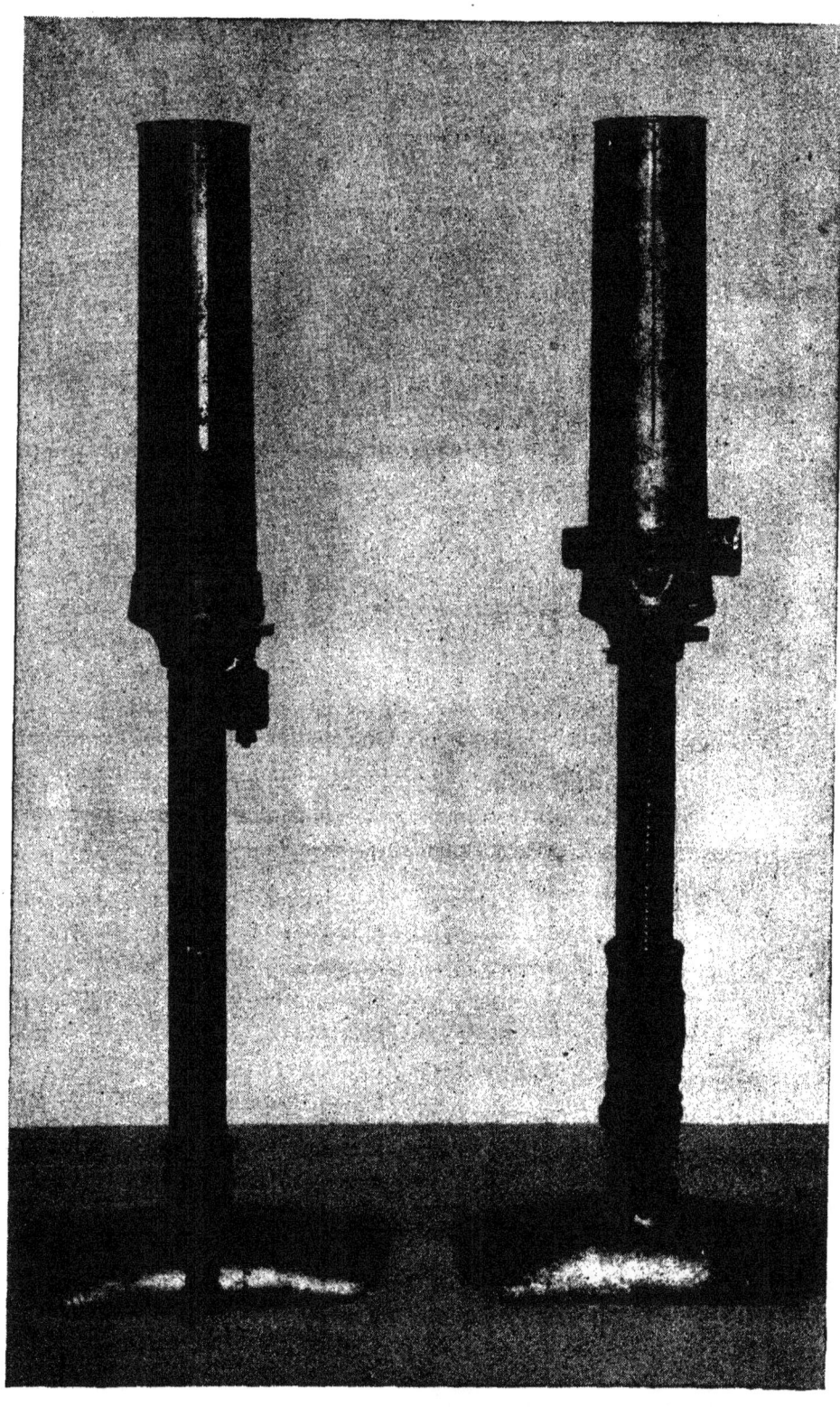

Figure 10.—Model 89 (1929) 50-mm grenade dischargers.

The weapon fires most effectively when held at a 45-degree angle; a version of the model found on Attu had a bubble-leveling device to indicate the 45-degree position. To fire the weapon with HE shell the safety pin is removed. The shell then is dropped down the barrel to the firing-pin housing where it remains until fired. When the lanyard is pulled, cogs in the trigger move the mainspring housing forward by engaging cogs in the front of it, thus causing the mainspring to be compressed. As this action occurs, the sear engages against the cocking lug of the firing-pin shaft. A continued pull on the trigger allows the sear to become disengaged from the cocking lug, and the compression of the mainspring upon thus being released sends the firing pin forward to set off the propelling charge. Loading and firing Model 91 (1931) hand grenades are accomplished in the same manner.

A new type sight for the Model 89 grenade discharger has been developed by the Japanese, although no specimen of the device thus far has been captured.

Inside the new sight there is an indicator, suspended by a pin at the top of the gauge housing. The indicator is a weight which swings freely through an arc limited to 45 degrees by lugs at each end. When the grenade discharger is held at the proper firing angle of 45 degrees, the gauge-housing cover reflects the image of the indicator through a window, enabling the gunner to see the indicator without changing his position.

Changes in deflection are made by turning the drift-adjustment knob at the rear of the gauge housing. This knob rotates the base of the traversing bar. On top the traversing bar is a V-shaped groove which serves as a sight through which alignment on the target is accomplished.

When the weapon is aimed, deflection is set on the drift scale. The tube then is pointed in the direction of the target, and the angle of 45 degrees is assumed by bringing the index on the indicator and the line on the vision window into coincidence. The sighting line on the traversing bar then is aimed at the target. Subsequent changes in deflection are made by turning the drift-adjustment knob.

Ammunition

The Model 89 (1929) HE shell fired by the discharger weighs one pound, 12 ounces. It is painted black, and has a quarter-inch red band at the head and a slightly larger yellow band around the center of the shell. The shell consists of a fuze, body, and propellent assembly. The fuze is a point-detonating type equipped with a safety pin, and is armed by setback and centrifugal force when the shell is fired.

The body of the projectile is made of steel and holds 0.31 pound of explosive filler. The propellent assembly includes a percussion cap, the propellent powder, and a copper rotating band. The whole propellent unit is joined to the shell body by a screw thread and is ignited when the firing pin hits the percussion cap.

Figure 11.—Model 91 (1931) HE grenade (left), and Model 89 (1929) 50-mm shell (right).

The Model 91 (1931) hand grenade, fired from both the Model 89 and the Model 10 dischargers, has two parts—the body and a base which contains propellant and primer. If thrown by hand, the propelling charge may be removed. To use in the discharger the safety pin is removed, the grenade placed in the barrel, and the trigger pulled.

Chemical Warfare Use

The 50-mm incendiary grenade also is fired from the dischargers. It is a cylindrical sheet-metal tube, with a hemispherical nose, covered with clear lacquer. Around the side are four silver-foil discs, each covering seven holes through the casing. The base is of metal, threaded to receive the same propellent charge as that used in the Model 91 grenade. The incendiary version weighs 1.25 pounds and contains an incendiary mixture of 0.67 pound. The charge is ignited by two black-powder pyrotechnic trains that run through the base of the grenade and are actuated by the flash of the propellant.

A Japanese 50-mm phosphorus smoke grenade has been found in recent operations. It is similar in some respects to the Model 91 (1931) HE grenade since it consists of a nose fuze of comparable design and action as well as a propellent unit suitable for projecting from a 50-mm discharger. Since the fuze can be activated by a blow on its head as well as by the shock of discharge, the grenade can be thrown by hand.

The grenade has a fuze covered by a brass safety cap, which is held in position by a double-pronged brass safety pin with an attached string finger loop. The fuze projects from the necked head of the smooth, unpainted brass body. The propellent unit is of blackened steel, having six equally spaced ports at the side and a visible percussion cap at the base. This unit is located at the bottom of the grenade and screwed into a threaded recess.

Before the grenade is inserted into the barrel of the discharger, the fuze must be armed by screwing home the striker pin. Then the safety pin is removed, leaving the safety cap loosely held at the groove in the fuze body. On discharge, the striker sets back on the percussion cap, which in turn ignites the delay pellet. After the delay period, the burning train reaches the black powder composition in the base of the pellet and initiates the intermediary pellet, which functions as the burster. The white phosphorus container presumably is shattered and forced out with the grenade head, thus scattering the contents. Even if thrown by hand, it is necessary to leave the propellent unit in place to retain the burster unit.

Specifications of the grenade are:

```
    Weight complete.............................................19 oz.
    Weight of propellent unit...................................2.97 oz.
    Weight of WP container (filled).............................8.93 oz.
    Weight of WP filling........................................6.09 oz.
    Over-all length.............................................5.71 in.
    Diameter of grenade body...................................1.958 in.
```

Three specimens of a smoke shell were captured in the Lae-Salamaua area. The shell is fired from a rifled barrel as in the Model 89 grenade discharger. It is nose-fuzed, using the Model 89 time fuze. The propulsion apparatus utilizes holes in the base of the shell for the escape of gases from the ignited propellant. The design provides for the ignition and base ejection in mid-air of a smoke case containing a hexachlorethane-zinc filling. The shell is painted black, with a red ring on the tip signifying that it is filled. There are two white bands, one in the rear of the shoulder and the other in front of the driving band, with Japanese characters stencilled between them.

Specifications of a shell are:

Total weight (with fuze hole plug)	29.75 oz.
Weight of fuze	5.93 oz.
Weight of black powder in primer	0.012 oz.
Weight of propellant (NC powder)	1.22 oz.
Weight of ignition mixture	0.06 oz.
Weight of smoke mixture	3.57 oz.
Weight of smoke mixture container (empty)	2.1 oz.
Length without fuze hole plug	4.42 in.
Length fuzed	6.15 in.
Caliber	1.969 in.
Diameter of front band	1.957 in.
Diameter in rear of front band	1.930 in.
Diameter of driving band	1.955 in.
Diameter at base of propellent unit holder	1.956 in.
Width of driving band	0.606 in.
Thickness of shell wall	0.116 in.

Smoke composition:

Hexachlorethane	40.5%
Zinc dust	4.5%
Zinc oxide (oxygen by difference)	48.5%
Zinc chloride	6.5%
Iron	Trace

The intended use of the projectile is uncertain. The small quantity (102 gm) of smoke composition would not enable the shell to be used efficiently for smoke screening. Its use for observation or signalling purposes is more probable. If burst above the jungle canopy it possibly could be employed to indicate targets for air support.

A grenade discharger, tentatively identified as a Model 99 (1939), has been reported. It is believed that this weapon has been designed to fire a new finned bangalore torpedo. The weapon weighs 39.7 pounds and has a maximum range of about 300 yards. The torpedo, which has an over-all length of 6.5 feet, weighs 19.2 pounds and contains a bursting charge weighing 4.7 pounds.

Light Mortars

Model 98 (1938) 50-mm Mortar

The Model 98 (1938) 50-mm mortar probably was designed primarily for attacks on small pillboxes and weapon emplacements. The most distinctive feature of the weapon is that it fires a powerful stick bomb, and the range is regulated by varying the depth to which this stick is permitted to slide down the barrel of the piece. This variation is accomplished by a device consisting of a clamp, scale, and locking screw. The clamp is attached to the muzzle of the tube, and by expanding or contracting the scale, which is graduated into 60 units, entry of the projectile into the barrel can be controlled.

Transport of the weapon is by pack or motor vehicle. One complete mortar, with its accessories, can be packed in two boxes and carried by a single animal, while 20 complete outfits can be transported in a truck. For short distances, the weapon sometimes is transported by the crew, usually with the tube group and base plate disassembled.

Figure 12.—Model 98 (1938) 50-mm mortar. Bipod clamp on center of tube connects bipod legs. Note traversing arc at forward end of base plate and scaled muzzle clamp for regulating range.

Figure 13.—Stick bomb fired from Model 98 (1938) 50-mm mortar. Insert shows bomb in mortar tube ready for firing.

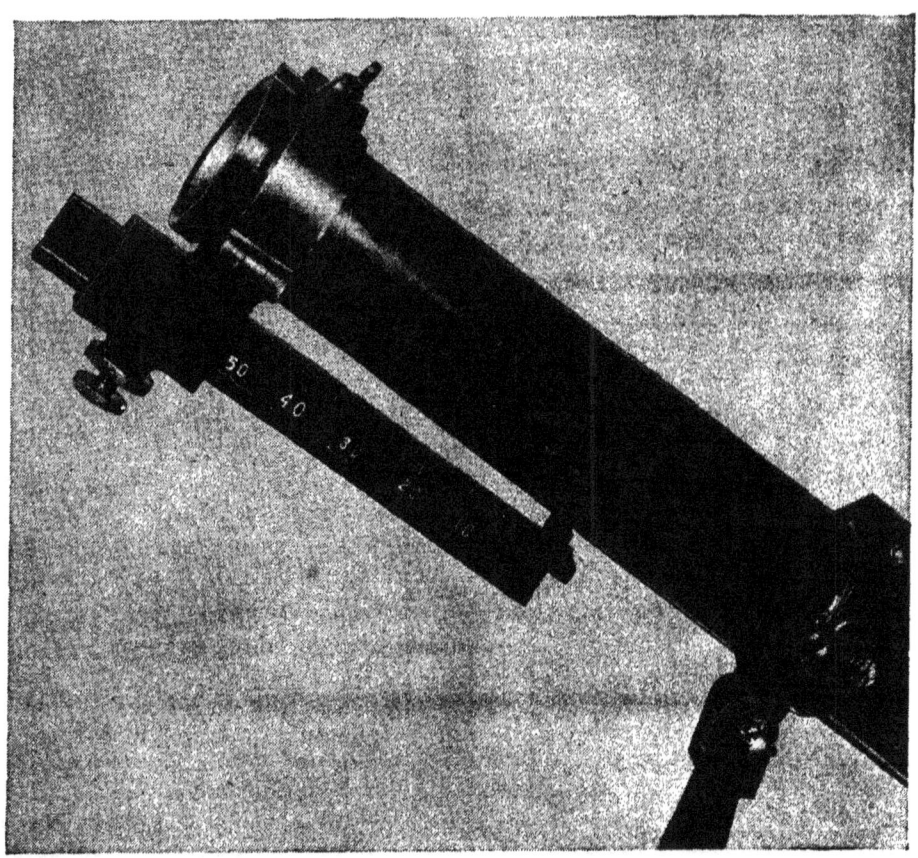

Figure 14.—Muzzle clamp of Model 98 (1938) 50-mm mortar. By means of scale, distance to which stick bomb is inserted in tube is controlled to regulate range.

Figure 15.—Front of base plate of Model 98 (1938) 50-mm mortar showing details of traversing arc and attachment of bipod legs.

Specifications of the weapon are:

Weight of mortar (complete)	50 pounds.
Internal length of barrel	25 inches.
Traverse	10 degrees, right and left.
Elevation	40 degrees (fixed).
Weight of bomb with stick	14 pounds.
Weight of explosive filling	5 pounds.
Dimensions of bomb head	4½ x 4½ x 6 inches.
Thickness of bomb casing	3/16 inch.
Length of stick	20 inches.
Diameter of stick	2 inches.
Maximum range with discharger bomb	440 yards.
Maximum range with demolition tube	320 yards.

The tube assembly of the mortar consists of the tube, baseplate, and bipod. The tube is a steel cylinder, 25.35 inches long and weighing 16.3 pounds. It has an ignition aperture, fitted with a cover and a sighting groove at the muzzle which aligns with the upper groove of the bipod clamp to form a sighting line. The breech, which constitutes the base of the tube, connects the latter with the base plate. The bipod clamp is fastened to the center of the tube and connects the bipod legs. The clamp also is fitted with a lock plate for the attachment of an ignition cord.

The base plate of the weapon is 31.2 inches long, 13.6 inches wide, and weighs 33 pounds. A traverse arc is recessed into the forward end of the plate, and movement of the bipod along this arc gives a traverse of 10 degrees right or left of center.

With the use of a propellent charge, the mortar fires a stick bomb, consisting of a steel plate box, filled with a bursting charge of picric compound cast in blocks, attached to a cylindrical, hardwood stick. A demolition tube also may be fired. This consists of a primary tube filled with a fuzed explosive to which is affixed a second tube equipped with fins to provide stability in flight.

The propellant consists of one or more increments of fine black powder. These are of either 25- or 35-gram weight, and are packed in silk bags 75- or 85-mm long. The bags are pushed down into the base of the mortar barrel with a cleaning rod until they touch the breech and are close to the ignition aperture. A friction-type igniter or primer then is fitted into the ignition aperture.

Figure 16.—Top view of tube of Model 98 (1938) 50-mm mortar. Note ignition aperture and cover (lower right), bipod and muzzle clamps, and sighting notch and line.

Two pull-type igniters are fitted into the base of the bomb, and the attached lanyards are tied to the bipod clamp. When the bomb is fired, these lanyards operate pull-igniters which activate the time fuze of the bomb, with a reported delay of 7 seconds. If the demolition tube is fired, it is projected in the same fashion. With either type of ammunition, the recoil of the weapon is quite violent, and considerable movement of the piece results.

Precise Japanese instructions have been issued in regard to the emplacement of the mortar. A board is placed under the base plate, and base plate stakes are driven into the ground to secure a firm foundation. If necessary, sandbags are placed on top of the plate to steady it. After the base plate is properly placed, the tube group is aligned with the center line of the base plate. In order to check the level, a plumb is suspended from the plumb hook on the bipod clevis.

The following special precautions in the use of the Model 98 50-mm mortar are emphasized by the Japanese: (1) Connect the primer and the slow-burning fuze. After the joint has been closed, wrap it several times with rubberized tape. This prevents the safety-fuze igniter and propellent charge flames and gases coming in direct contact with the primer. (2) Do not allow the propellent charge to gather moisture when using in rainy weather or after the tube has been washed with water. Carefully clean the tube bore with dry cotton waste. Do not allow moisture drops to remain in the tube base. If the propellent charge becomes damp, it will cause misfires, a change of burning speed, or incomplete combustion which not only will decrease the projectile's accuracy, but will lessen fixed range. The shell even might drop directly in front of the discharger and inflict casualties on the mortar crew. (3) Cleaning of the tube must be done carefully after each round. (4) Before inserting the propellent charge, the gunner always must examine the tube bore to make certain that no water drops or burning powder-bag residues remain. (5) During severe hot weather, the gunner periodically must check the tube for over-heating when using a combination of large propellent charges. If the tube is over-heated, there may be an unexpected ignition of the propellent charge at the time of insertion. When operating under conditions where the tube is easily over-heated, wash the tube frequently with water or cool the tube under the ignition aperture with wet cotton waste. (6) Remove the safety pin from the fuze of the finned demolition tube immediately before loading. After the safety pin has been removed, do not revolve the safety vane. Violation of this precaution may cause improper functioning of the fuze or it may be the cause of an unexpected detonation. (7) Do not bend the fins of the demolition tube or the vanes of the fuze safety vane. Bending of the fins will create an ineffective trajectory. (8) Do not load projectiles which are covered with dirt and sand. This will cause excessive wear and damage to the bore. (9) Never use a propellent charge of fine grain powder of more than 50 gm for the finned demolition tube. The tube resistance is limited. Propellent charges (fine grain powder) of more than 100 gm are not used for discharger bombs. The resistance of the discharger bomb-rod is insufficient and will be easily damaged. Do not use a propellent charge (fine grain powder) of more than 120 gm in the Model 98 discharger.

Japanese List of Accessories for Model 98 (1938) 50-mm Mortar

Article	Number	Construction and Use
Swabbing Rod	1	Used to clean the tube bore. It consists of a brush and a handle. The handle is in two parts, A and B, which are used after coupling.
Cleaning Rod	1	Cloth is tied to one end and is used to clean the tube bore. It consists of two parts, A and B.
Powder Scale	1	A brass cylinder which can be expanded or contracted and which is used to measure fine grain powder. The expanding or constricting tube has graduations of 5 gm units—from 5 to 50 gm.
Pliers	1	Used to cut wire.
Plumb	1	Used to sight the target of the discharger and to check the base-plate level.
Muzzle Cover	1	Cover of cotton material made to fit the tube and used to cover the muzzle.
Base Plate Stake Covers	4	Covers of cotton material which fit over both ends of the base-plate stakes and are used to carry them.
Fuze Kit	1	Made of cloth and holds 26 fuzes (igniter, slow-burning fuze, safety-fuze igniter joined together).
Tool Kit	1	Made of cotton material which holds the pliers, 7-mm screw driver with handle attached, 10-mm screw driver with handle attached, one ignition cord "A", and two ignition cords "B".
Fuze Box	1	Holds the fuze kit and igniters.
Powder Bag Box	1	Holds the propellent charge.
Range Control Device Box	1	Holds the range control device.
No. 1 Box	1	Holds the base plate, tube, swabbing rod, and cleaning rod. It is easily transported by pack animal.
No. 2 Box	1	Holds the remaining accessories and is easily transported by pack animal.

Model 11 (1922) 70-mm Mortar

The Model 11 (1922) 70-mm mortar is exceptional among Japanese mortars in that, although a muzzle-loading weapon, it has a rifled bore. The Japanese marking is "11th Year Model High-Angle Infantry Gun". A monopod, similar to the support of the U. S. 4.2-inch chemical mortar, is another outstanding feature.

Total weight of the weapon is 133.75 pounds, of which 99.5 pounds represent the weight of the base plate. The traverse of the piece is 410 mils (23 degrees), and its elevation is 661 to 1,370 mils (37 to 77 degrees).

A gunner's quadrant is used to lay in the weapon. It has a level vial, actuated by a knob, a movable arm, and a fixed elevation scale. The elevation scale is graduated in half-degree units from 0 to 55 degrees. The movable arm has a vernier scale which permits readings of $\frac{1}{16}$th degree.

Before the weapon can be fired, by means of a lanyard attached to a striker arm, a latch pin on the breech end of the tube must be set in its recess. HE shell is fired. The complete round consists of a fuze, the shell body, and the propellent-charge assembly. The fuze is a point-detonating type, consisting of a two-piece brass body, a booster cup, a detonator holder, and a washer.

The steel shell body is threaded at the top to receive the fuze assembly, and at the bottom to accommodate the propellent-charge assembly. It

Figure 17.—Left side of Model 11 (1922) 70-mm mortar. Tube is supported by elevating screw. Note traversing wheel and base-plate spades. Insert shows 70-mm mortar shell and fuze.

is marked with a white band near the base and a red band at the nose. The propellent-charge assembly consists of the percussion cap, the propellent powder, and an expanding copper rotating band. The propellent charge is ignited when the firing pin hits the percussion cap. The propellent gases expand the copper rotating band against the rifling in the interior of the barrel; the rifling causes the projectile to rotate and thus increases the accuracy of its flight. The projectile is 8.62 inches long and 2.18 inches in diameter; the complete round weighs 4 pounds, 10.8 ounces.

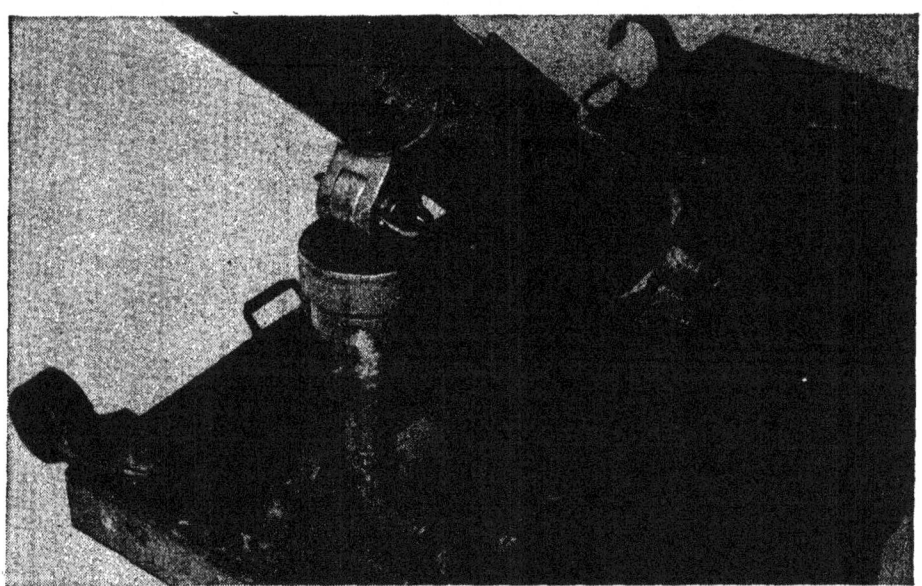

Figure 18.—Elevating screw of Model 11 (1922) 70-mm mortar. Note trunnioning of tube.

Figure 19.—Top view of base plate of Model 11 (1922) 70-mm mortar.

70-mm Barrage Mortar

The Japanese 70-mm barrage mortar was first encountered on Attu. It consists of a smooth-bore tube, 4 feet long, the steel base plate of which is fastened by two bolts to a wooden block, 10 x 12 x 8 inches. A large iron spike on the under side of the wooden block is thrust into the ground to anchor the weapon, and the angle at which this is done controls elevation. The wooden block absorbs some of the shock of firing and prevents the mortar from embedding itself into the ground.

In addition to use against ground targets, the mortar has been employed as an antiaircraft weapon and is reported to have a maximum vertical range of approximately 4,000 feet. A curious mounting of the weapon in a Japanese plane also has been reported, with a plane of the "Dinah" type firing three rounds rearwards from a single mortar to ward off an attack by U. S. fighters. An 81-mm version of the weapon recently has been encountered, apparently designed for the same tactical use as the 70-mm model.

The shell which is fired by dropping it down the mortar tube contains seven parachute bombs, each 3 inches long and $11/16$ inch in diameter. The propellent charge ignites a delay powder train, which subsequently ignites an expelling charge within the shell when it reaches the standard altitude.

Figure 20.—70-mm barrage mortars found on Kiska. Elevation is controlled by angle at which anchoring spike is thrust into ground. Note steel base plates bolted to wooden blocks.

Figure 21.—70-mm barrage mortar.

Figure 22.—Operation of shell of 70-mm barrage mortar.

The expelling explosion causes the projection of the parachute bombs, each of which is supported by a rice-paper parachute. At the same time, a larger parachute opens, tilting the main container to ensure scattering of the seven bombs. The jerk caused by the opening of the bomb parachutes initiates the action of the detonating fuzes of the sensitive pull-igniter type, which are equipped with phosphorus-coated string and delay elements. The blast effect of the parachute bombs is severe, and the danger area is about 10 to 20 yards in radius.

Five rounds have been fired in a test, with the mortar at a 75-degree elevation. One round failed to eject the parachute bombs because of the malfunction of the delay-train ignition. The shells were quite noisy in flight and tumbled considerably, with the smoke of the black-powder delay train plainly visible. The releasing burst occurred in 7 to 8 seconds at altitudes of 1,520 to 1,660 feet, and the shell cases hit the ground close to the firing position. All inert components of the round drifted to the ground within 30 seconds, and the bombs drifted nearly a half mile, landing at intervals of about 30 yards.

Shells for the 81-mm barrage mortar recently were found on Leyte. An HE cylinder, attached to two parachutes, is propelled. A 45-second delay train is ignited in the shell which slowly descends. Detonation occurs after a fall of from 500 to 1,000 feet, or the shell may be exploded if a 33-foot cord attached to the igniter is struck by a plane.

Specifications are:

Total weight of shell	3 lbs. 14 oz.
Over-all length	21.063 in.
Diameter of shell body	1.496 in.
Diameter of cylinder parachute	11.968 in.
Diameter of igniter parachute	15.984 in.

Model 97 (1937) 81-mm Mortar

Japanese infantry units often are equipped with 81-mm mortars. The Model 97 (1937) 81-mm mortar is very commonly used and is referred to by the Japanese as an "Infantry Gun". A captured piece, which has been studied in detail, was marked "Model 97 High-Angle Infantry Gun". The weapon was manufactured in 1942 in the Osaka Army Arsenal.

Although the Japanese weapon closely resembles the U. S. 81-mm mortar, M1—there are several identifying features by which the two can be distinguished. The adjusting nut of the Japanese mortar is on the right bipod leg, while the sight is on the left. Other differences are the buttress-type threads on the traversing and elevating screws of the Japanese weapon, as well as the use of welding to fasten bipod legs to the clevis joint and grease fittings dissimilar to those used by the U. S. model.

Figure 23.—Model 97 (1937) 81-mm mortar. Cross-leveling device is on the right bipod leg.

Figure 24.—U. S. 81-mm mortar M1 (left); Japanese Model 97 (1937) 81-mm mortar (right).

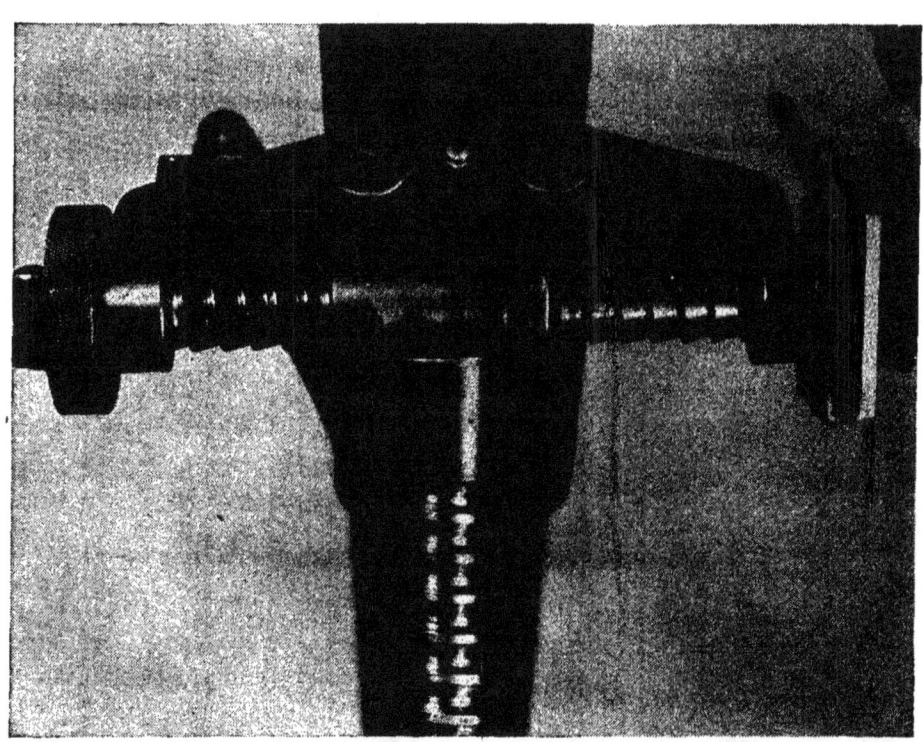

Figure 25.—Buttress-type threads on elevating and traversing screws of Model 97 (1937) 81-mm mortar. Note details of T-joint.

The Model 97 is a smooth bore, muzzle-loading weapon. It has a fixed firing pin in the breech assembly, and the percussion of the propelling cartridge of the mortar shell against the firing pin propels the shell from the mortar. As many as six propellent increments can be attached to the fins of the mortar shell for the purpose of increasing the range.

Specifications of the weapon are as follows:

Over-all length	56 inches.
Length of tube, including base cap	49½ inches.
Length of bore	45¾ inches.
Diameter of bore	82 mm.
Thickness of tube wall	0.275 inch.
Length of base plate	16½ inches.
Width of base plate	26½ inches.
Total weight	145 lbs. 2 oz.
Weight of tube	45 lbs. 9 oz.
Weight of bipod	47 lbs. 14 oz.
Weight of base plate	51 lbs. 12 oz.
Range, maximum, approximate	3,000 yards.

The collimator sight for the Model 97 Japanese mortar is heavier and more complicated than that utilized on the U. S. 81-mm mortar M1. The Japanese sight examined was made entirely of steel, except for the brass bushings used for the elevating and cross-leveling screws. A U. S. M4 sight may be fitted to the Japanese weapon by shimming the sight bracket slightly.

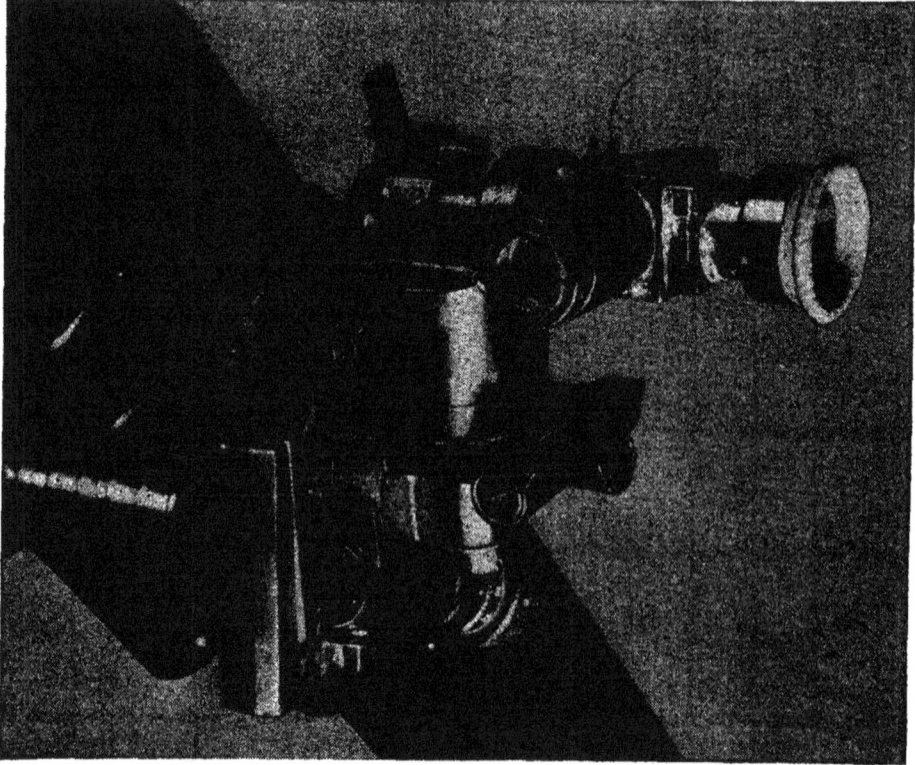

Figure 26.—Sight of Model 97 (1937) 81-mm mortar.

The Model 97 mortar examined had an extension fitted to the sight, raising the latter to the level of the muzzle of the mortar. This extension probably was added to permit sighting of the weapon when it was deeply dug in or slightly defiladed. Elevation scale of the sight is graduated in 50-mil intervals from 700 to 1,600 mils, and a micrometer drum enables elevation readings to be made to the nearest mil. The collimator can be traversed in a full circle, and the azimuth scale is calibrated in 100-mil graduations in two sections of 3,200 mils each. As in the case of elevation, a micrometer drum permits azimuth readings to be made to the nearest mil. There is a throw-out lever for rapid traverse of the collimator, which may be placed at an angle of elevation and locked in position by a series of meshing notches. There are no open sights for rough laying of the piece.

Ammunition

Ammunition recovered for the Model 97 thus far is usually the Model 100 (1940) HE shell. This shell is 12.87 inches long and weighs 6.93 pounds, 1 pound of which is the weight of the TNT filler. The fuze is of the instantaneous type, which can be set for delay action, however, by the insertion of a delay pellet in the fuze nose prior to firing. The shell can be fired in the U. S. 81-mm mortar M1, but the range will be about 10 per cent shorter than achieved with the U. S. M43 and M43A shells.

A firing test of Japanese shells in the U. S. 81-mm M1 weapon gave the following results that cannot be regarded as wholly conclusive in view of deterioration of the shells.

Tentative firing table in U. S. 81-mm M1 mortar

Yards	Elevation (degrees)	Charge (no. of increments)
3,125	46	6
2,840	50	6
2,745	55	6
2,540	60	6
2,200	65	6
2,200	48	4
2,100	55	4
1,925	60	4
1,675	65	4
1,415	70	4
1,440	46	2
1,410	50	2
1,225	55	2
1,175	60	2
980	65	2
880	70	2
750	75	2
505	45	0
490	55	0
420	65	0

U. S. M43 shells can be fired from the Japanese Model 97 mortar, but firing tests resulted in 25 per cent misfires, most of which were caused by the sharp firing pin. U. S. ammunition gave greater range than the Japanese, however, because of its greater powder pressure.

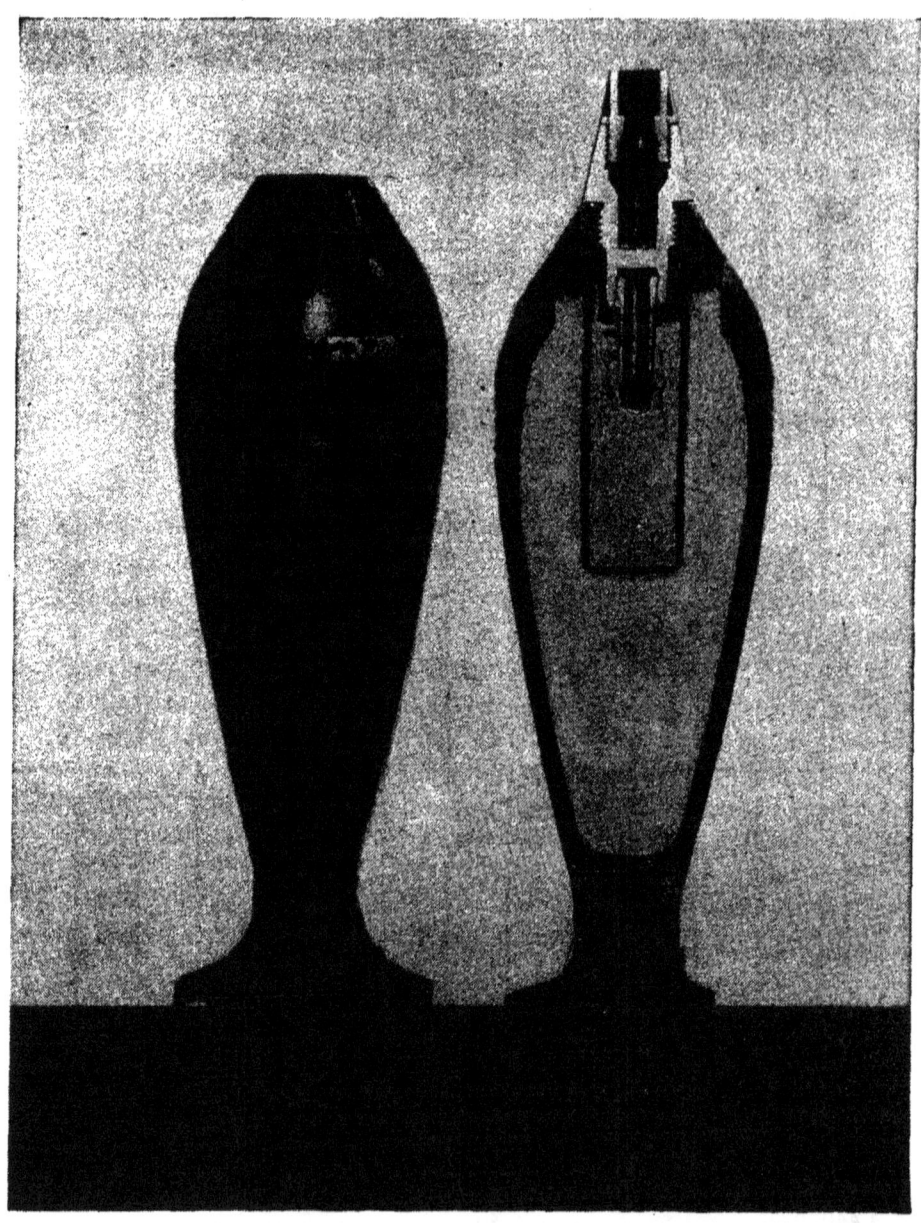

Figure 27.—Model 100 (1940) 81-mm mortar shell.

A firing test with Japanese ammunition resulted in more than 50 per cent misfires, but this test was not conclusive since the ammunition had deteriorated as a result of contact with water. It had been packed in plain wooden boxes, with ignition cartridges and increments in ordinary paper bags. Another lot of ammunition, most of which had been packed in boxes that were carefully lined with waterproof paper, with the ignition cartridges and increments in waterproof bags, produced only 15 per cent misfires, almost all of which occurred with rounds not so packed. Most of the misfires were attributable to the ignition cartridge bases remaining in the mortar.

The Japanese generally were poorly prepared for the proper packaging of ammunition at the start of the war. Ammunition of all kinds was packed in wooden boxes with fillers to hold it in position, and only the most rudimentary protection against moisture was provided by tarring joints and knotholes and occasionally wrapping rounds in wax paper for additional waterproofing. In view of the faulty packaging, it was common for 50 per cent to 90 per cent of hand grenades and mortar shells to fail to function. Now, however, the Japanese are utilizing metal and asphalt-impregnated paper linings for their ammunition containers, and consequently deterioration has been materially lessened.

Japanese Firing Table for Model 97 (1937) 81-mm Mortar

Elevation	Primary propellent charge cartridge only	1 increment	2 increments	3 increments	4 increments	5 increments	6 increments	8 increments
83½	100							
82¾	110	200						
82½		210	300	400				
82¼	120							
82		220	320		500			
81¾		230		420				
81½	130		340	440				
81¼		240			550			
81	140	250	360	460				
80½		260		480				
80¼		270	380	500	600	700		
80	150							
79¾		280	400					1,000
79½	160	290			650	750		
79¼			420					1,050
79		300		550			900	
78¾	170		440			800		1,100
78½					700			
78¼		320	460				950	1,150
78	180			600		850		
77¾								1,200
77½		340	480		750		1,000	
77¼	190					900		1,250
77			500	650			1,050	
76¾		360			800			1,300
76½	200					950		
76¼							1,100	1,350
76		380						

Japanese Firing Table for Model 97 (1937) 81-mm Mortar

Elevation	Primary propellent charge cartridge only	1 increment	2 increments	3 increments	4 increments	5 increments	6 increments	8 increments
75¾	210			700	850			
75½			550		-	1,000	1,150	1,400
75	220	400						1,450
74¾				750	900	1,050	1,200	
74½								1,500
74¼	230	420	600				1,250	
74					950	1,100		
73¾							-	1,550
73½			440	800			1,300	
73¼	240					1,150		
73					1,000			1,600
72¾			650					
72½	250	460					1,350	1,650
72¼				850		1,200		
72					1,050			
71¾	260	480					1,400	1,700
71½						1,250		
71¼			700					1,750
71				900	1,100		1,450	
70¾	270	500						
70½						1,300		1,800
70¼							1,500	
70	280							1,850
69¾				950	1,150			
69½			750			1,350		
69¼							1,550	
69	290							1,900
68¾					1,200	1,400		
68½				1,000			1,600	
68¼		550						1,950
68	300							
67¾						1,450		
67½			800		1,250		1,650	2,000
67¼								
67				1,050				
66¾						1,500		
66½					1,300		1,700	
66¼	320							
66				850				2,100

Elevation	Primary propellent charge cartridge only	1 increment	2 increments	3 increments	4 increments	5 increments	6 increments	8 increments
65½		600				1,550	1,750	
65¼				1,100				
65					1,350			
64½						1,600	1,800	
64¼								2,200
64	340		900					
63¾				1,150	1,400			
63½						1,650	1,850	
63¼								
63								
62½		650			1,450		1,900	2,300
62¼								
62	360		950	1,200		1,700		
61½							1,950	
60¾					1,500	1,750		2,400
60¼				1,250			2,000	
59¾	380							
59½			1,000					
59¼					1,550	1,800		
59		700						
58¾								2,500
58½				1,300				
57¾						1,850		
57½					1,600			
56¾								2,600
56½	400		1,050					
56¼						1,900		
56				1,350				
55¼					1,650			
55		750						
54½								
54¼						1,950		
54								2,700
53	420			1,400	1,700			
52½			1,100					
51¾						2,000		
50							2,300	2,800
45	440	790	1,130	1,460	1,770	2,070	2,340	2,850
MV	67m/sec	92m/sec	113m/sec	130m/sec	145m/s	160m/sec	172m/sec	196m/sec

Model 99 (1939) 81-mm Mortar

The Model 99 (1939) 81-mm mortar also is very widely used by Japanese forces. It differs from the Model 97 in the shortness of its tube, which is only 21.75 inches as compared with 45¾ inches of the Model 97. Of much greater significance, however, is the difference in the method of firing. Whereas the Model 97 has a fixed firing pin in the base cap, the Model 99 has its firing pin affixed to a camming shaft that extends outside the base cap of the mortar. This shaft must be struck a sharp blow with a mallet to drive it inward so as to force the firing pin against the primer of the propellent cartridge. The primer ignites the propellent charge of the cartridge, which in turn ignites the powder increments attached to the fins.

The weapon fires with an exceptionally loud report and a pronounced muzzle flash. When the firing-pin cam shaft is struck, the camming shaft spring is extended. When it snaps back into its original shape, it withdraws the camming shaft thus bringing the firing pin down into the base cap in position for the next shot.

Figure 28.—Model 99 (1939) 81-mm mortar. Tube is only 25.5 inches long (over-all). Note base-plate spade and ribs to permit mortar to dig in firmly.

Figure 29.—Model 97 (1937) 81-mm mortar (left); Model 99 (1939) 81-mm mortar (right).

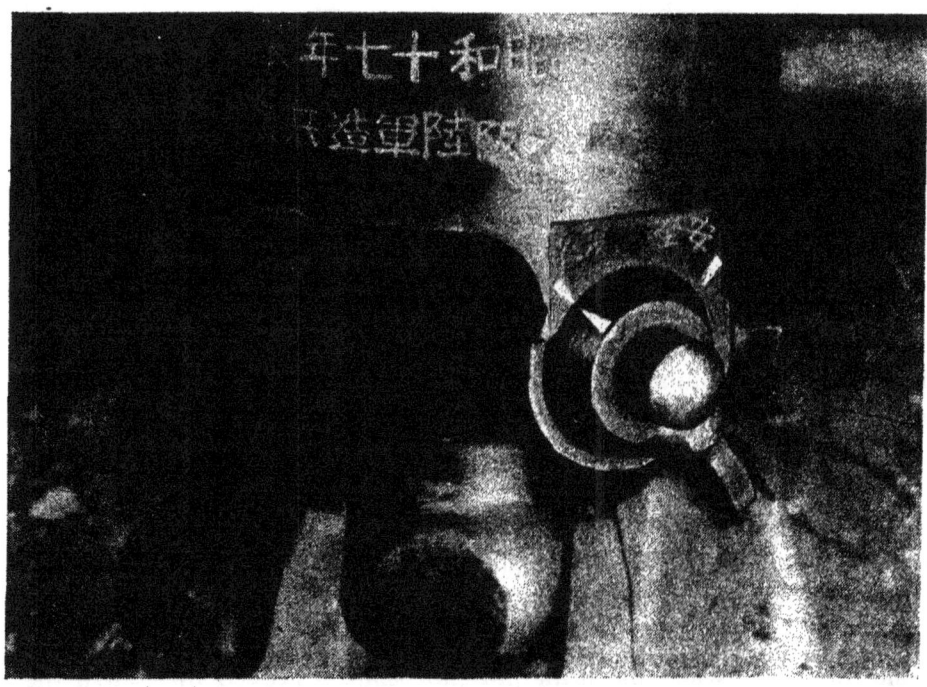

Figure 30.—Base cap of Model 99 (1939) 81-mm mortar. Striking firing-pin cam shaft at lower right of tube fires the piece.

Differences between the Model 99 and the U. S. 81-mm mortar M1 are pronounced. In addition to the different methods of firing, the tube length of the Japanese weapon is only about half that of the U. S. mortar (25.5/59.5 inches). The Japanese weapon also employs a turn-buckle for cross-leveling instead of an adjusting nut and connecting rod, and its recoil mechanism also differs from that of the U. S. piece. Finally, the Japanese base plate has only one socket for the base-cap knob, and it is not provided with a sighting line.

Specifications of the Japanese Model 99 (1939) 81-mm mortar are as follows:

Weight of mortar tube	17.5 pounds.
Weight of bipod	16.5 pounds.
Weight of base plate	18.3 pounds.
Weight of complete mortar	52 pounds.
Length mortar tube	21.5 inches (interior).
Length mortar tube	25.5 inches (over-all).
Elevation: Minimum	35 degrees.
Maximum	50 degrees.
Traverse right or left	60 mils.
Size of base plate	14.25 x 14.25 inches.
Range	500-2,200 yards.

The mortar can be disassembled into three units—the tube, the bipod, and the base plate. When in firing position, the mortar tube is attached to the bipod by a clamp. It then is fastened to the base plate by the insertion of the spherical knob on the base cap into the socket on the plate and rotating the mortar 90 degrees right or left.

The tube is smooth bored, and its interior surface is carefully finished. Tolerance between the wall of the tube and the bourrelet of the shell is very close, thus preventing the shell from striking the firing pin with sufficient percussion to detonate the primer. On its outside surface the tube has a sighting line and quadrant seat at the muzzle end.

The base cap of the tube is hollowed and threaded to screw on to the breech end of the tube which it thereby seals against gas leakage. The cap terminates in a spherical knob, which locks into the socket of the base plate and is bored and threaded axially to receive the firing pin and the base cap plug. When in place the firing pin is held retracted into the base cap by the camming-shaft spring, being compressed between the camming shaft and the camming-shaft lock.

When the change lever is turned to "safe", the firing pin is locked "down", the firing-pin cam is locked "out", and the mortar will not fire. When the change lever is turned to "fire", the pin is in the "down" position, but the cam now has free movement. If the cam shaft now is struck with a block or mallet, the firing pin is forced to the "up" position firing the round. It should be noted that the change lever cannot be turned from "safe" to "fire" when the firing-pin cam shaft is pressed in. But if the change lever is turned from "fire" to "safe", with the firing-pin cam

Figure 31.—Top view of tube of Model 99 (1939) 81-mm mortar.

shaft pressed in, the firing pin is locked in the "up" position, and the round will be fired automatically when dropped down the tube.

The legs of the bipod, made of tubular steel, are mounted on the elevating screw housing by a clevis joint. They terminate in thin steel plates which have single-pointed spikes on the underside. The spread of the legs is limited by a chain which has a spring attached to one end to relieve the shock of firing. A buffer system incorporated in the bipod gives a recuperation of 2 inches. The recoil cylinders are filled with light grease or heavy oil.

The base plate, made of pressed steel, has a series of ribs and braces

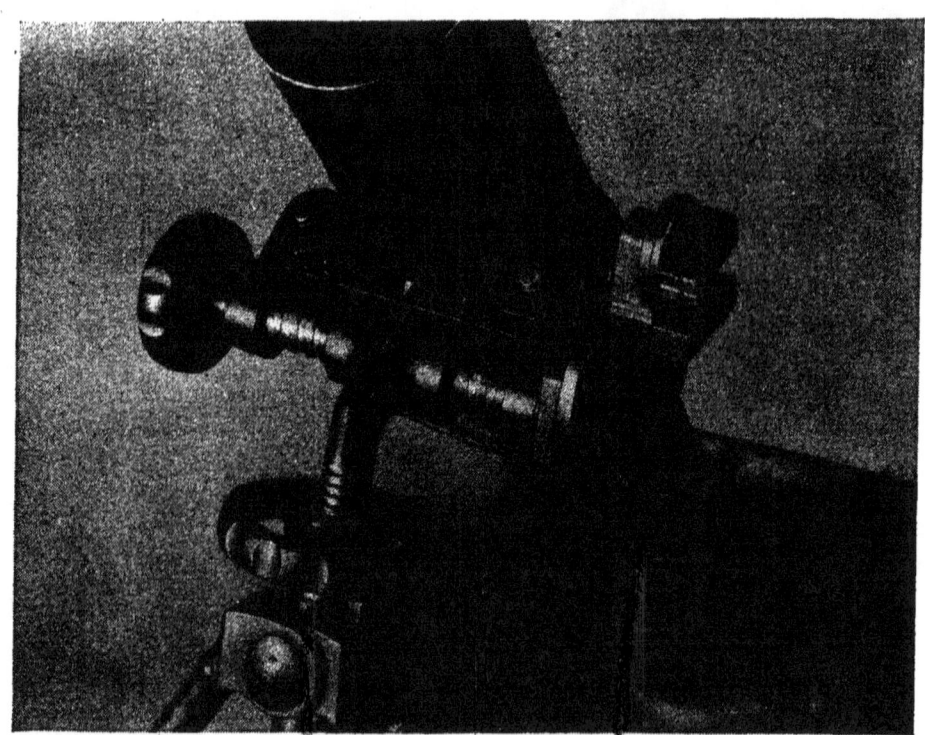

Figure 32.—Traversing and elevating screws of Model 99 (1939) 81-mm mortar. Note clevis joint mounting bipod legs on elevating screw housing.

Figure 33.—Sight for Model 99 (1939) 81-mm mortar. Note elevation and cross-leveling bubbles and elevation scale.

welded on the underside to allow it to dig into the ground when the piece is fired. On the topside of the plate, in the center, is a circular depression into which the base-cap knob fits when the mortar is mounted in firing position. A carrying handle is attached to the rear edge of the plate. Also, two small hooks are welded to the rear edge to permit the attachment of a carrying strap. Around the outer edge of the plate is a one-inch ridge, and on the lower front edge a hook is attached through which a small rod can be thrust and used for slight changes in base plate alignment.

A stability test of the Model 99 mortar, in which a total of 14 rounds were fired, produced no visible evidence of cracking or deformation of either base plate or bipod. The plate sank about 2 inches into the ground with the firing of seven rounds at alternate elevations of 45 to 75 degrees. Stability was very satisfactory when firing zone charges I to IV, but zones V to VI produced noticeable hop of the mortar and a sinking of the base plate.

The reported range of the weapon of about 2,200 yards has not been conclusively confirmed. The following results were achieved in a firing test that employed both Japanese ammunition and U. S. M43A.

FIRING TABLE

Range with Jap Ammunition	Range with U. S. M43A Ammunition	Elevation (degrees)	Charge (no. of increments)
2,200	2,530	45	6
2,040	2,340	56.2	6
1,700	1,900	45	4
1,580	1,715	56.2	4
1,000	1,275	45	2
900	1,100	56.2	2
450	515	45	0

Model 3 (1943?) 81-mm Mortar

Two specimens of the Model 3 (1943?) 81-mm mortar were captured in the Marshall Islands. They are marked "Model 3 81-mm Trench Mortar made in 1943, Yokosuka Navy Arsenal". Despite the model designation, the mortar is believed to be a forerunner of the Model 97 81-mm piece, the base plate of which can be used with the Model 3. The general appearance of the Model 3 is identical with that of the Model 97 (1937) 90-mm mortar.

The tube of the Model 3 has the same length as that of the Model 97, but on the former there are two collars machined on the forward portion of the barrel for securing the bipod clamp. The bipod of the Model 3 is constructed of light-weight tubing, and there is no cross-leveling device. Rough cross-leveling adjustment could be made, however, by breaking the bipod support and moving the leg on the low side inward. The threads of the traversing and elevating mechanisms are of the square type, rather than of the efficient buttress type utilized in the Model 97. No sight has been reported for the Model 3, and the sight for the Model 97 will not fit. The sight mount of the Model 3 is considered unstable.

The total weight of the Model 3 is 167 pounds. The tube weighs 47 pounds, the bipod 25 pounds, and the base plate 95 pounds.

Ammunition

The Model 3 8-cm shell recently has been identified for use in the 81-mm mortars. Shaped like the usual types of mortar ammunititon, this shell has three features which are new in Japanese mortar shells. The cylindrical initial propellent charge is held in position by a base screw, instead of the usual "shotgun shell" type of cartridge. Increments are in circular bags placed around the tail above the fins. Secondly, the shell has 12 short tail fins, instead of the six long fins found on other Japanese mortar shells. Thirdly, a new type of fuze, of the "time and percussion" type, is used with the shells. It is set for a predetermined time by rotation of a time ring in the lower part of the fuze.

On firing, set-back causes the time-train firing pin to function. This initiates the powder in the time-train ring and ignites the safety powder pellet, freeing the impact firing pin. Thus the fuze will function on impact if impact occurs before expiration of the set time. The time-setting can be eliminated altogether by turning the setting ring off the scale. It should be noted that the fuze is not interchangeable with fuzes used in other 8-cm mortar ammunition.

Ammunition for the Model 99 mortar is issued disassembled, but with all components packed in the same box. To prepare a round for firing, the plug is pulled from the booster cavity, and the fuze locked in place by screwing in the set screw located in the nose of the projectile. An ignition cartridge then is pushed firmly into place in the base, and the desired number of powder increment bags are placed between the fins. The fuze is covered with metal foil and has a projecting wire loop which operates as a tear-wire to aid in removing the foil. Misfires may occur with some frequency as a result of the base of the ignition cartridge remaining in the tube and preventing the next round from being properly seated.

A Model 100 (1940) fuze for 81-mm mortar shells recently has been identified. The fuze has three main parts—nose, body, and booster. It is made of brass with the exception of the striker-detonator assembly. The nose, which screws into the body and is held by a grub screw, contains the arming-firing device. A cavity behind the nose is covered with a perforated brass disk to distribute the flash from the detonator. In the bottom of the cavity is a cylindrical brass plug. This plug is pierced in the middle by a diametrical hole, while another hole, corresponding to the radius, enters at right angles. This second hole is filled with black powder which acts as a delay train. For instantaneous action the plug is turned so that the flash travels directly from the detonator to the booster without passing through the delay train. Turning the plug clockwise 90 degrees makes the flash travel through the delay-train hole prior to reaching the booster.

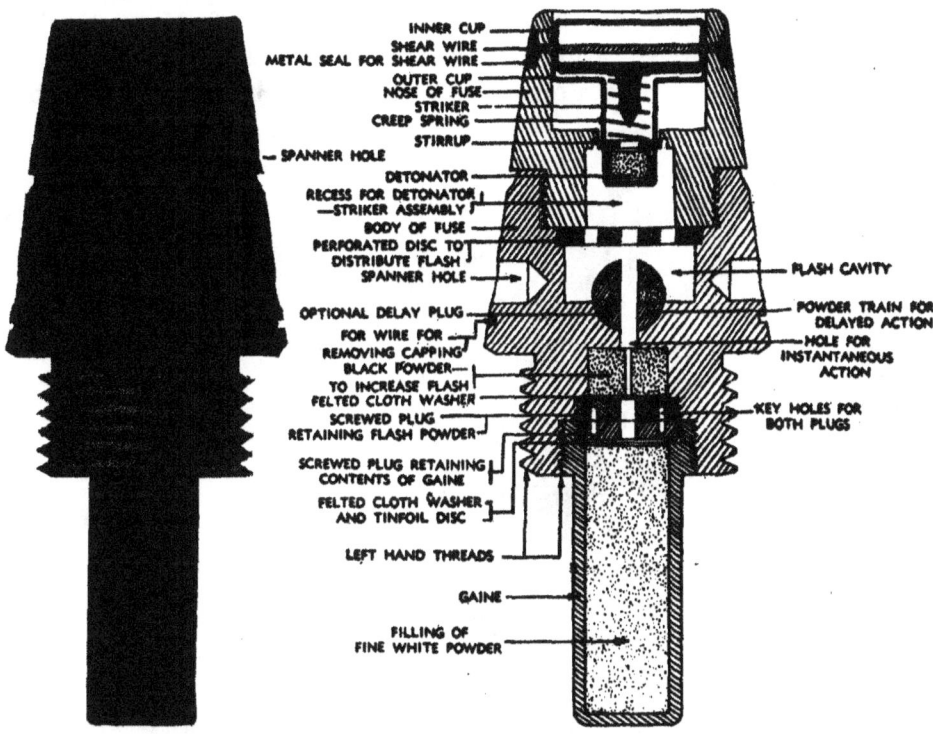

Figure 34.—Model 100 (1940) fuze for Model 3 81-mm mortar shell.

Model 94 (1934) 90-mm Mortar

The Model 94 (1934) 90-mm mortar is used by artillery mortar units. It is a smooth-bore, muzzle-loading weapon, with a fixed firing pin. An outstanding feature of the piece that distinguishes it from most other mortars used by modern armies is the recoil mechanism. This consists of two cylinders mounted on a one-piece U-shaped frame, which in turn fits

Figure 35.—Model 94 (1934) 90-mm mortar. Note recoil cylinders mounted on U-shaped frame.

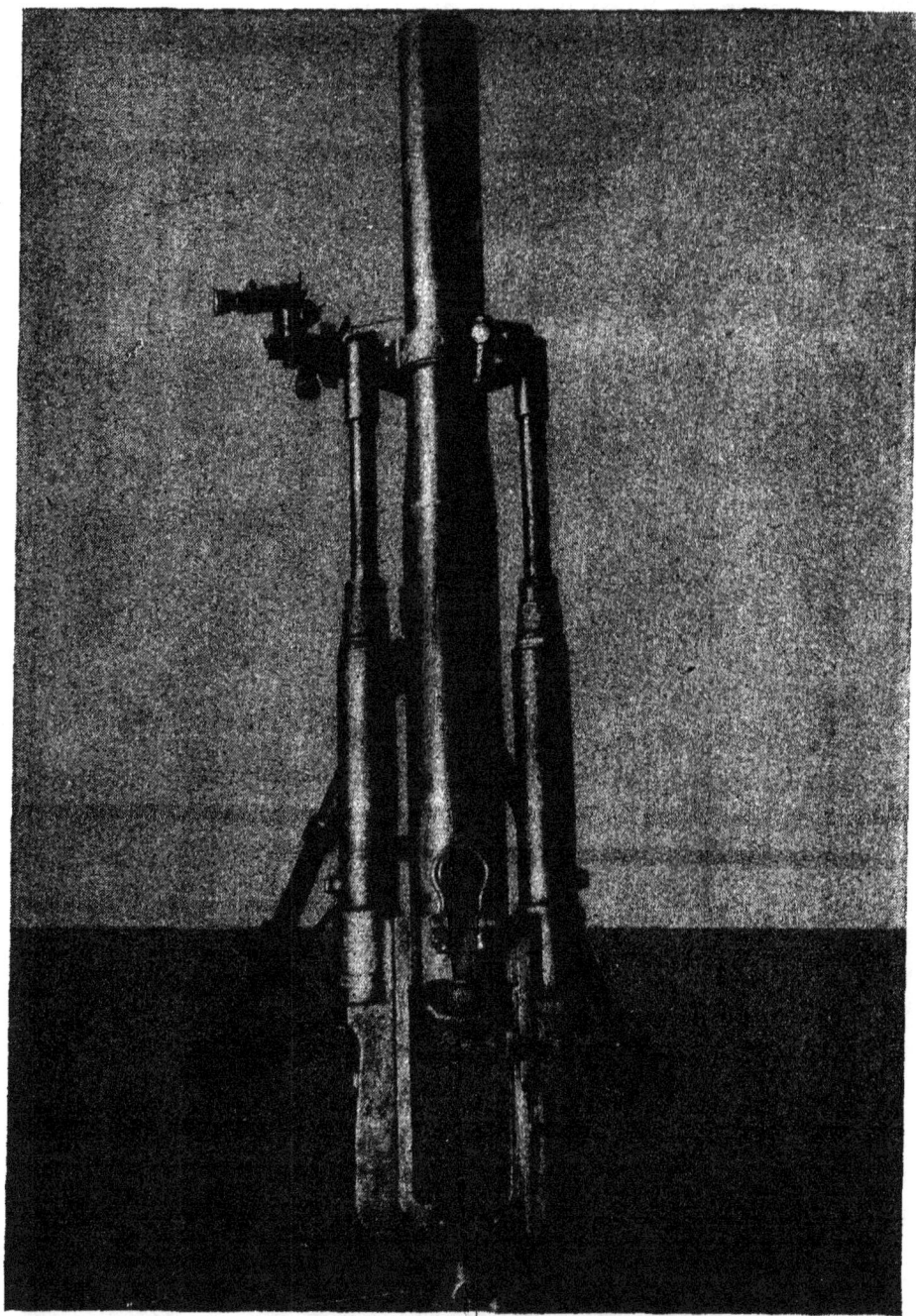

Figure 36.—Top view of Model 94 (1934) 90-mm mortar. U-shaped frame which holds tube and recoil cylinders fits into base plate by ball and socket mounting. Recoil mechanism makes up about 110 pounds of the total weight of the weapon.

into the base plate by a ball-and-socket arrangement. The tube is connected by a bar to the recoil cylinders, and the cylinders also are attached to bipod shock absorbers.

The weapon can be disassembled into four main parts—the tube assembly, recoil assembly, bipod assembly, and base plate. The barrel assembly consists of the tube, the breech ring, and the breech mechanism. This entire assembly can be removed from the recoil assembly by removing a U-shaped pin which locks it at the extension of the breech end. The frame, or yoke, is removed from the base plate by rotating it 90 degrees around its longitudinal axis to disengage the ball from the socket of the base plate. The bipod then is removed by unlocking the mortar clamp.

Figure 37.—Release of U-shaped pin permits removal of tube-assembly from yoke.

Specifications of the Model 94 are:

Over-all length of tube	4 ft. 2 in.
Length of tube interior	4 ft. 0 in.
Outside diameter tube at muzzle	103 mm (4.02 inches).
Outside diameter tube at base	116 mm (5.12 inches).
Bore diameter	90 mm (3.51 inches).
Weight of tube	76 lbs.
Size of base plate	2 ft. 5 in. x 1 ft. 6½ in.
Weight of base plate	92 lbs.
Weight recoil mechanism	110 lbs. (estimate).
Weight of bipod group	75 lbs.
Total weight	353 lbs.
Range	3,570 yards.

Two types of traversing gear have been distinguished for the Model 94. One has a traversing handwheel equipped with a crank, whereas the other is without a crank. Total traverse in both types is 177 mils (10 degrees). Elevation is accomplished by turning a crank at the junction of the bipod legs and the elevating screw. The cross-leveling device is a knurled nut and collar on the bipod leg.

The mortar is leveled and layed-in by the same procedure that would be utilized in firing the U. S. 81-mm mortar M1. The projectile is allowed to slide down the barrel, fins first, and it is fired by striking a fixed firing pin. At the signal to fire all crew members crouch below the muzzle of the weapon, for there is a great deal of flash, although the concussion is not excessive.

Tubes of mortars fired by dropping the shell down the tube were found cemented into the rock at strategic points on Peleliu. Retreating Japanese soldiers dropped shells from nearby caches into these tubes as they passed to lay down a barrage to cover their retreat.

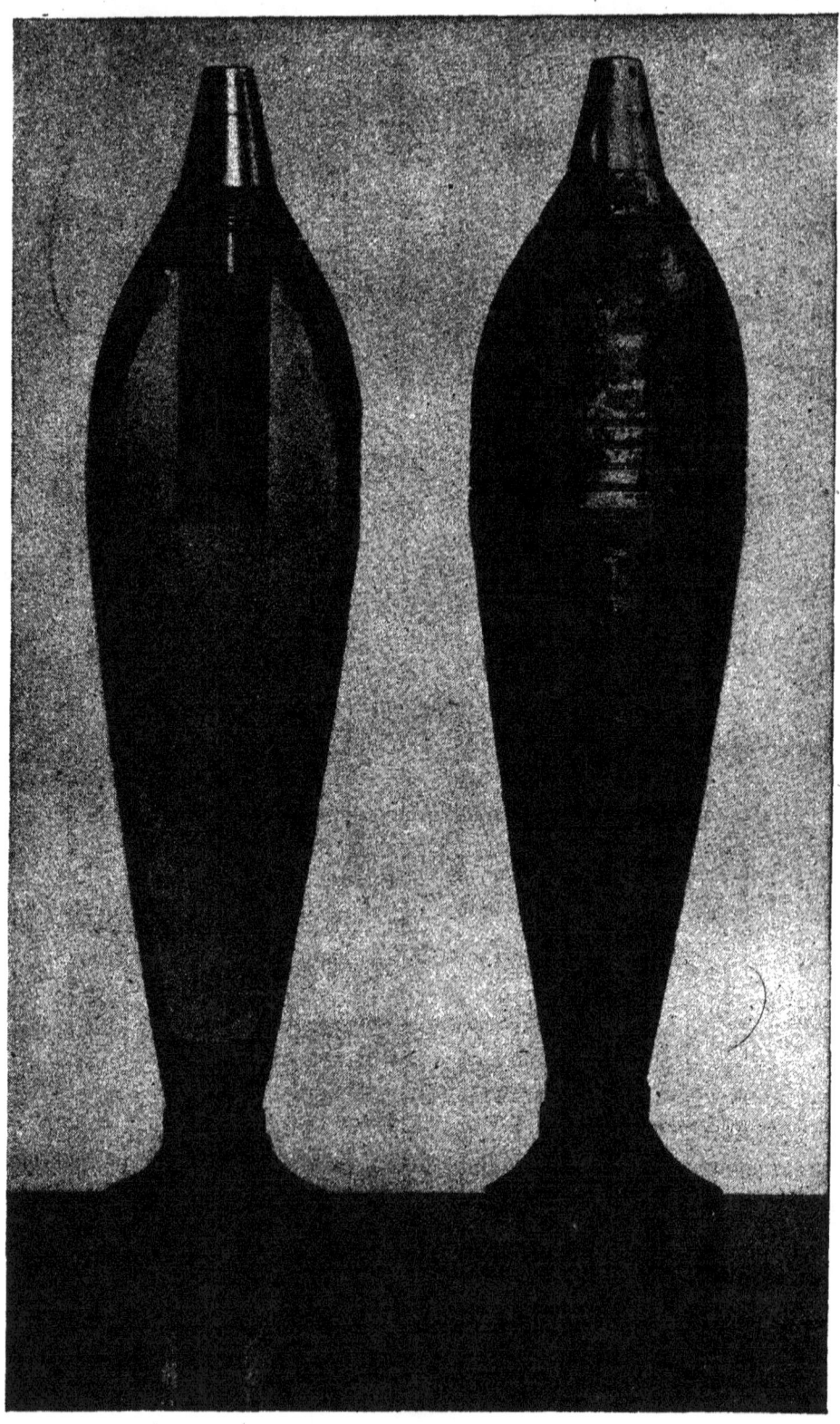

Figure 38.—90-mm mortar shell.

Ammunition

Both high-explosive and chemical shells are fired from the Model 94. The HE shell, which is 15.875 inches long over-all and has a maximum diameter of 3.537 inches, weighs 11 pounds, 2 ounces. Total weight of the explosive filling is 2 pounds, 5 ounces.

The body of the HE shell is painted black and has three color bands. A red band painted on the adapter of the shell assembly indicates that it is filled, and a white and a yellow band are painted respectively below and above the bourrelet. The white band indicates that the shell is made of steel, while the yellow indicates HE filling.

The approximately hemispherical nose of the shell widens out at the base of a parallel-sided bourrelet, 3.5 inches in diameter, in which there are four grooves of special shape to form gas-check rings. The body of the shell tapers away sharply towards the tail. Screwed into the base of the shell body is a tube 4.45 inches long and 1.28 inches in diameter. This tube has a threaded portion, 0.624 inch long, to screw into the base of the shell. The primary propellent cartridge fits inside this tube. Twenty-four holes, each 0.195 inch in diameter, are drilled laterally through the tube in six vertical rows of four each, and over every alternate row of holes is welded a steel bracket, shaped so as to form six tail fins, and retaining clips for the attachment of secondary propellent charges.

Screwed into the nose of the shell is a hollow steel adapter, threaded internally to take at its lower end a brass burster-container, 3.75 inches long and 1 inch in diameter. The adapter, which is retained in the bomb body by means of a grub screw, is closed with a fuze when prepared for firing or with a transit plug for shipment. Another grub screw in the adapter holds the fuze or transit plug in place.

The brass burster-container which screws into the adapter is painted internally and externally with dark purple lacquer. A copper container, formed by soldering together two cups, fits inside the burster-container and accommodates the lower part of the fuze. The burster-container is filled with a bursting charge of 42.15 grams of picric acid.

The fuze for the HE shell normally is instantaneous, but it can be converted for slight delay by the insertion in the body of a delay plug which makes the flash from the detonator pass through a powder train in the delay plug.

The fuze consists of a head, body, and booster, all made of brass. The body is threaded internally to accept the head in which are housed the firing mechanism and detonator. The base of the body of the fuze is internally screw-threaded to accept the booster. The over-all length of the fuze and booster is 3.75 inches, and maximum diameter is 1.25 inches. Total weight of the filled fuze is 184.73 grams (6.5 ounces).

The firing mechanism of the fuze consists of an anodised duralumin wind shield, a shear wire, a striker pin and base, a spiral spring and aluminum stirrup, and a detonator. All components are enclosed in a duralumin housing. The booster has a tubular brass body, 1.85 inches long, with an enlarged screw head (0.56 inch) for insertion into the base of the body of the fuze. The filled weight is 0.174 ounce. There are two increments, the upper one in the tube consisting of a small amount of fulminate of mercury, while the lower increment is pressed CE. The main explosive filling of the bomb comprises 2 pounds, 5 ounces of TNT, in the upper surface of which is a cavity to house the burster-container.

The primary cartridge is a purple, cardboard tube, rolled over at one end around a closing disc and contained at the other in a brass head. A thin, shorter cardboard tube is inserted inside the outer tube. A cardboard wad is pressed tightly into place in the lower end of the outer tube; this wad bears against the lower end of the inner tube. Concentric holes punched in the brass head and the cardboard wad form a chamber into which is pressed a copper percussion cap. The cap contains on its outside a brass cup over which is placed a brass sheet anvil with a central flash hole. The residue of a cap which had been fired showed traces of mercury upon analysis. It probably contained fulminate of mercury, potassium chlorate, and antimony sulphide. The cartridge itself is filled with thin bluish flakes of nitrocellulose plus diphenylamine and blue dye.

No fuze action takes place when the piece is fired. On impact, however, the windshield is crushed, breaking the shear wire and forcing the housing and striker downwards. The detonator continues on its forward course and impinges on the striker. The ensuing flash passes directly to the booster, or, if delay is desired, through the optional delay plug en route to the booster.

The fuze is packed in a soldered tinplate container with a screwed-on lid. It is held rigid by two wooden blocks shaped to fit into the container and internally recessed to take the base and nose of the fuze.

Out of a total of 15 HE rounds fired in a test, there were eight misfires. Two rounds fired with faulty ignition traveled only 50 to 200 yards respectively, while two others yielded only about half the anticipated range. The large proportion of faulty ammunition was believed attributable to unsatisfactory packaging methods employed by the Japanese.

The incendiary shell, which also is used with the Model 94 90-mm mortar, is 16 inches long and weighs 11.6 pounds. In appearance it is quite similar to the U. S. 81-mm mortar projectile. It can be distinguished by four colored bands painted around its circumference. There is a red band just below the fuze, and a blue band halfway between the fuze and the bourrelet. Halfway between the bourrelet and the fin assembly is a yellow band, and there is a white band at the junction of the shell body and the fin assembly.

White phosphorus, carbon disulphide, and about 40 impregnated cylindrical rubber pellets constitute the incendiary filling of the shell. A 2.8-ounce bursting charge scatters the mixture upon impact.

Model 97 (1937) 90-mm Mortar

A newer Japanese 90-mm mortar is the Model 97 (1937), a Stokes-Brandt type similar in appearance to the U. S. 81-mm mortar M1 and the Japanese Model 97 (1937) 81-mm piece. It is believed that the 90-mm weapon has been introduced more recently than its model number would imply. A captured specimen was marked "Model 97 Light Trench Mortar, Manufactured in 1942, Osaka Army Arsenal".

The Model 97 is approximately 120 pounds lighter than the Model 94 (1934) 90-mm mortar. This weight saving has been effected largely by the elimination of the recoil mechanism, weighing 110 pounds, with which

Figure 39.—Model 97 (1937) 90-mm mortar with sight mounted. Note heavily ribbed base plate and three base-plate sockets to receive ball of tube base cap.

Figure 40.—Model 97 (1937) 90-mm mortar (left); Model 94 (1934) 90-mm mortar (right). The Model 97 is about 120 pounds lighter than the Model 94 mainly because of the elimination of recoil cylinders on the Model 97.

Figure 41.—Lower bipod leg and foot of Model 97 (1937) 90-mm mortar.

the Model 94 is equipped. The bipod assembly of the Model 97 is 14 pounds lighter. There is a cover for the level on the yoke of the Model 97 which is not on the earlier weapon, and the sliding bracket of the Model 97 is hinged to permit its easy removal from the leg of the bipod, whereas it is integral on the Model 94.

Certain compromises in material and workmanship have been made in the manufacture of the Model 97. The bipod feet and chain hooks are held to the legs of the bipod by pins, probably sweated on with solder, whereas on the Model 94 they are welded. No welds are polished on the Model 97, although no indications of fractures have been reported despite the poor quality of the welding. The adjusting nut, sliding bracket, and handwheels of the Model 97 are made of steel, rather than brass which was utilized in the earlier model.

Maximum range of the Model 97 is the same as that of the Model 94 —approximately 4,150 yards. Other specifications are:

```
Over-all length of barrel.........................4 ft. 4¾ in.
Length of barrel, interior........................4 ft.
Outside diameter of barrel at muzzle..............111 mm.
Outside diameter of barrel at base................111 mm.
Diameter of bore.................................. 90 mm.
Weight of barrel.................................. 80 pounds.
Size of base plate................................2 ft. 5 in. x 1 ft. 6½ in.
Weight of bipod group............................. 61 pounds.
Total weight......................................233 pounds.
Thickness of tube wall............................0.275 inch.
```

Medium and Heavy Mortars

12-cm Mortar

A number of medium and heavy mortar models are in use by the Japanese Army. A 12-cm (4.7-inch) model is described by the Japanese as having an over-all length of 4 feet, 11.9 inches, and a bore length of 4 feet, 5.6 inches. The total weight of the weapon is reported to be 548½ pounds, of which 176 pounds represent the weight of the tube, 99 pounds the bipod, and 207.9 pounds the base plate.

The weapon allegedly can be fired by dropping the shell down the tube to strike a fixed firing pin, or it can be trigger fired. Elevation of the piece, accomplished by adjustment of the bipod legs, ranges from 800 to 1,422 mils; traverse, at a 45-degree elevation, is 180 mils and at 70 degrees 210 mils. Maximum range of the piece is reported to be 4,900 yards.

Capture of a Model 2 (1942) 120-mm mortar recently has been reported from Leyte. This weapon is a smooth bore, muzzle-loading type which, except for the firing mechanism, closely resembles the conventional Stokes-Brandt 81-mm mortar. The bipod and cradle of the two types of mortars are identical, except for size and the fact that the bipod legs can be removed as a unit from the cradle of the 120-mm mortar. The large, ribbed base plate has only one socket for the spherical projection on the barrel.

The base plate is very heavy and is fitted with four carrying handles. The sight bracket fits the standard mortar sight. The barrel is heavily reinforced at the muzzle and has two raised ribs midway of the barrel, between which the barrel clamping collar is held. The firing mechanism is similar to that used on the type 99, 81-mm short mortar. After the weapon has been loaded, a plunger, which projects upward from the mortar breech, is struck with a mallet or similar instrument, thus camming out the firing pin and firing the mortar. A safety lock is fitted on this firing plunger. The mortar examined was manufactured at Osaka Arsenal in 1943.

The ammunition is of the conventional streamlined, fin-stabilized type. It uses the ignition cartridge and powder-increment type of propellant. The round uses the standard type 100 mortar fuze and weighs 26.4 pounds. Two rounds of ammunition are packed in a wooden box, lined with asphalt impregnated paper. The ignition cartridges are assembled into the rounds as packed, the fuzes are packed in tear-top cans, and the doughnut-type increments are packed in tar-paper bags.

Model 93 (1933) 15-cm Mortar

A Model 93 (1933) 15-cm mortar also is described by the Japanese. It is a muzzle-loading weapon, the barrel of which is not rifled but bored to receive a shell with six bourrelets. The weapon is intended for vehicle transport, but in view of the lack of a carriage it is difficult to move.

Reported, but unconfirmed specifications are:

```
Over-all length of tube.................................5 ft. 4 in.
Length of bore..........................................4 ft. 11 in.
Weight of tube..........................................242 pounds.
Actual bore.............................................5.94 inches.
Actual diameter of shell................................151.6 mm.
```

The weapon, which has a reported range of 2,290 yards, fires a shell which carries the propellent and primer charges. The total weight of the complete shell is 44 pounds, of which 14.6 pounds constitute the weight of the bursting charge.

Model 95 (1935) 15-cm Mortar

The Model 95 (1935) 15-cm mortar is served by a crew of 11 men. According to the sight setting it has a maximum range of 2,270 yards. The tube is 4 feet, 2 inches long, and weighs 222.2 pounds. The bipod assembly weighs 134.2 pounds, and the base plate about 220 pounds. The weapon can be elevated from 45 to 80 degrees, and the total traverse is 14 degrees left or right.

Model 97 (1937) 15-cm Mortar

The Japanese Army, which has relied heavily upon the trench mortar for fire support, also has developed the Model 97 (1937) 15-cm mortar.

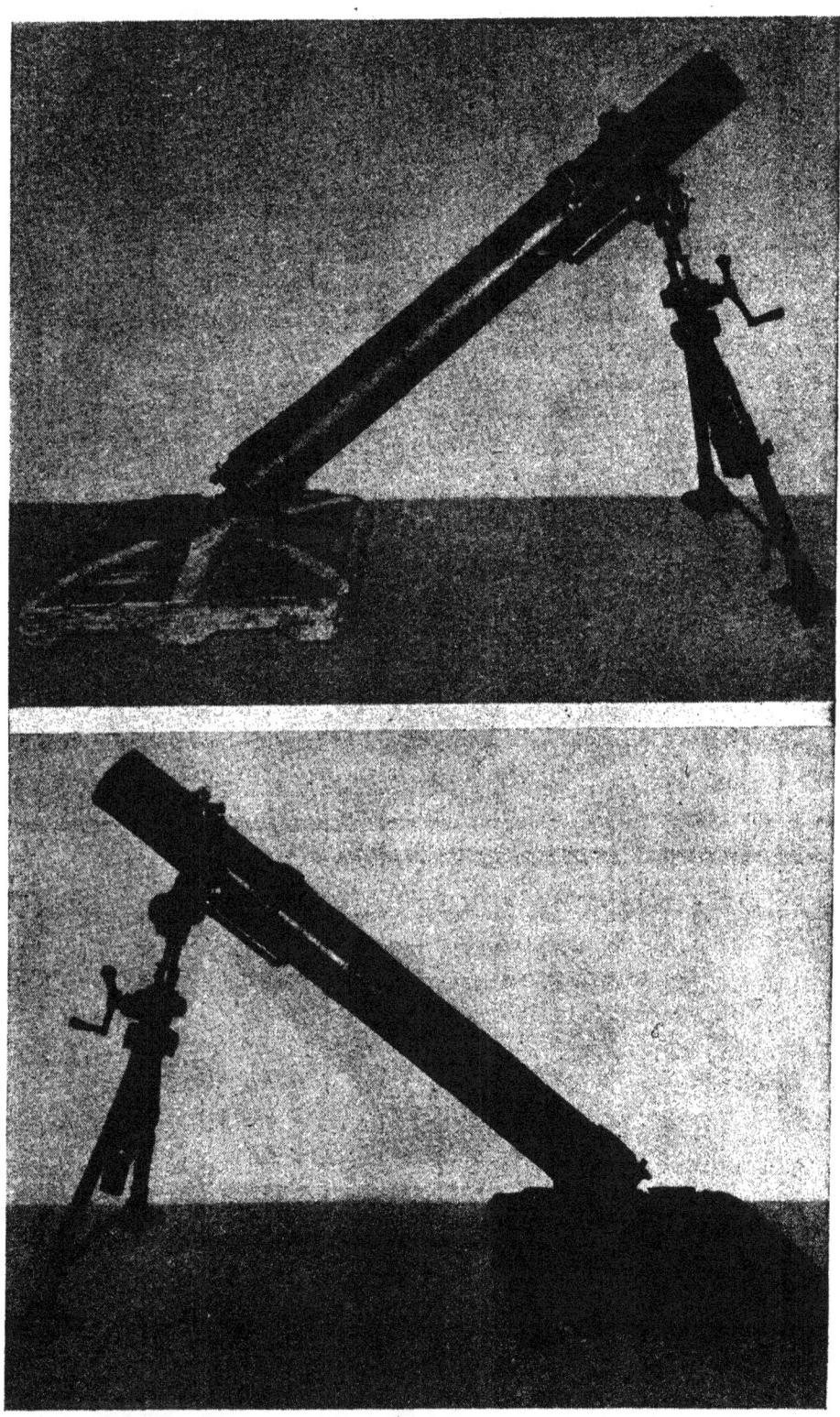

Figure 42.—Model 97 (1937) 15-cm mortar. Maximum range is reported to be about 2,190 yards. Note firing-pin cam shaft in base cap, reinforcing muzzle band, and 3-power panoramic sight mounted on left side.

Although this weapon has not yet been widely used, it may be encountered more extensively again by U. S. troops at any time in the near future.

Called a "medium" mortar by the Japanese, this Model 97 (1937) 15-cm weapon is a conventional smooth-bore, muzzle-loading, bipod-mounted mortar of sturdy construction. On Peleliu Island, the weapon was emplaced in a concrete pit with the muzzle level with the top of the pit.

This 15-cm mortar, which resembles in design the standard U. S. 81-mm mortar, weighs 770 pounds complete with sight, and fires a conventional-type high-explosive shell weighing approximately 57 pounds.

The weapon is sighted by means of a 3-power panoramic elbow telescope, and the Japanese claim it will throw a projectile a maximum 2,190 yards. Bursting radius of the shell is reported to be 65 feet, with some fragments thrown 100 feet farther.

For transport the mortar, including the sight, breaks down into five component parts as follows:

	Pounds
Tube	257
Base plate	337
Bipod and elevating gear	100
Traversing gear, shock-absorbers, and mortar clamps	74.5
Sight	1.5

The tube is 75.37 inches long and has a reinforcing muzzle band, while the heavy, ribbed-steel base plate measures 47.75 inches by 35.5 inches.

The weapon is assembled, adjusted for fire, and operated similarly to the U. S. 81-mm mortar. However, the firing mechanism resembles that of the Japanese Model 99 81-mm mortar, using a firing-pin cam shaft built into the base cap, rather than a fixed firing pin.

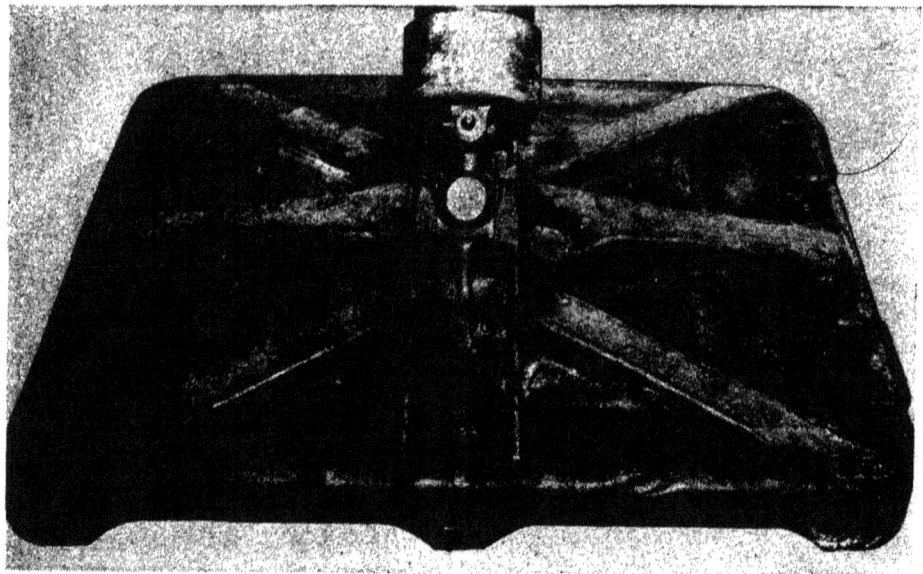

Figure 43.—The heavy, steel base plate of the Model 97 (1937) 15-cm mortar weighs 337 pounds.

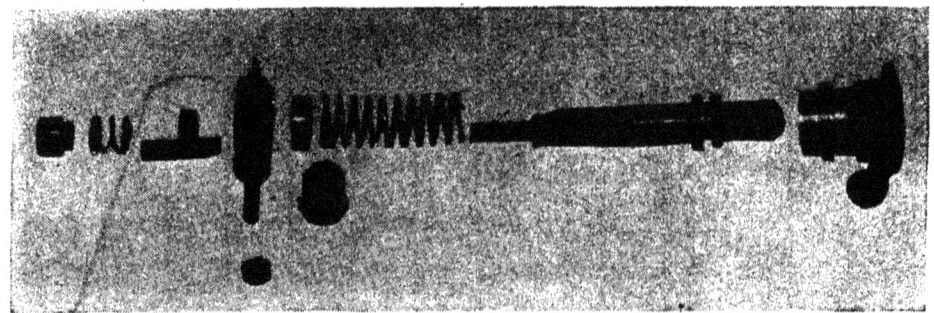

Figure 44.—Firing-pin assembly of Model 97 (1937) 15-cm mortar.

The Japanese are known to have another Model 97 150-mm mortar which is yet to be encountered. It is reported to weigh 1,540 pounds and have a maximum range of 3,840 yards. There is a possibility that this mortar may be installed on a mobile mount.

Other Models

A Model 99 (1939) short-barreled medium mortar of 15-cm caliber also recently has been reported. It weighs 341 pounds and fires a shell weighing 59.4 pounds. Its range is reported to be approximately 755 yards, and the muzzle velocity is 301.7 feet per second.

A 15-cm steel artillery mortar also has been reported, although no comprehensive data can be given as yet. The weapon apparently is used by artillery mortar battalions, with four pieces assigned to each component company. The weapon, which is breech-loading, has a very short barrel with a bore of 149.1 mm.

Japanese mortars of 155-mm (6.1 inches) caliber have been reported from Palau but no details are available as yet.

15-cm Mortar Projectile and Model 93 (1933) Fuze

A Japanese 15-cm mortar shell recently has been examined. It has the same tear-drop shape as the 81-mm projectile. Its main body is a machined cast steel container, threaded internally at the nose to receive the fuze adapter and internally at the tail to receive the propellent tube. The bourrelet consists of five well machined bearing surfaces separated by shallow grooves. Specifications of the projectile are:

```
Over-all length (less fuze)..........................28¾ in.
Diameter of bourrelet...............................15.0 cm.
Thickness of case....................................7/16 in.
Outside diameter of booster tube....................1 3/16 in.
Inside diameter of booster tube......................1 in.
Length of booster tube..............................3 11/16 in.
Length of propellent tube excluding forward threaded portion......7 13/16 in.
Outside diameter of propellent tube..................2 1/8 in.
Inside diameter of propellent tube...................1 1/2 in.
Diameter of tail....................................14.9 cm.
Thickness of fins...................................5/32 in.
Width of fins......................................1 15/16 in.
Length of fins.....................................6 1/2 in.
Length of propellant...............................5 1/2 in.
Diameter of propellant.............................1 1/2 in.
Length of brass head...............................13/16 in.
Weight of complete round less fuze and propellant..........56.5 oz.
Weight of main charge...............................9.0 oz.
Weight of propellent cartridge loaded................6 oz.
Weight of propellent cartridge empty.................4 oz.
Weight one increment................................3.3 oz.
Weight of propellant................................2.3 oz.
Weight of booster charge.............(½ oz. tetryl, 1 oz. picric acid.)
```

The Model 93 (1933) combination fuze is used with the shell. It is an impact-firing, point-detonating fuze, with a brass body and booster. The portion of the fuze exposed when the fuze is in the projectile is in the shape of a truncated cone. The cup assembly which houses the striker and primer is aluminum, as is the striker itself. A copper shear wire runs diametrically through the cup assembly above the striker. Both the upper and lower sections of the fuze body have two diametrically opposed spanner notches. Specifications are:

```
Over-all length....................................3 13/16 in.
Maximum diameter...................................1 ¼ in.
Weight complete....................................5.8 oz.
Length of fuze (visible when installed)............1 ½ in.
Diameter of fuze base threads......................15/16 in.
Threads per inch on fuze base L/H..................13.
Length of upper fuze body..........................1 in.
Diameter of external threads in upper fuze.........¾ in.
Threads per inch in upper fuze body R/H............20.
Length of striker seat.............................½ in.
Diameter of threads of striker seat................½ in.
Threads per inch of striker seat L/H...............20.
Length of booster..................................1 3/8 in.
Diameter of booster threads........................17/32 in.
Threads per inch on booster L/H....................28.
Length of delay housing............................¾ in.
Diameter of delay housing..........................15/32 in.
Weight of black powder delay.......................0.35 gm.
Weight of mercury fulminate in booster.............2.44 gm.
```

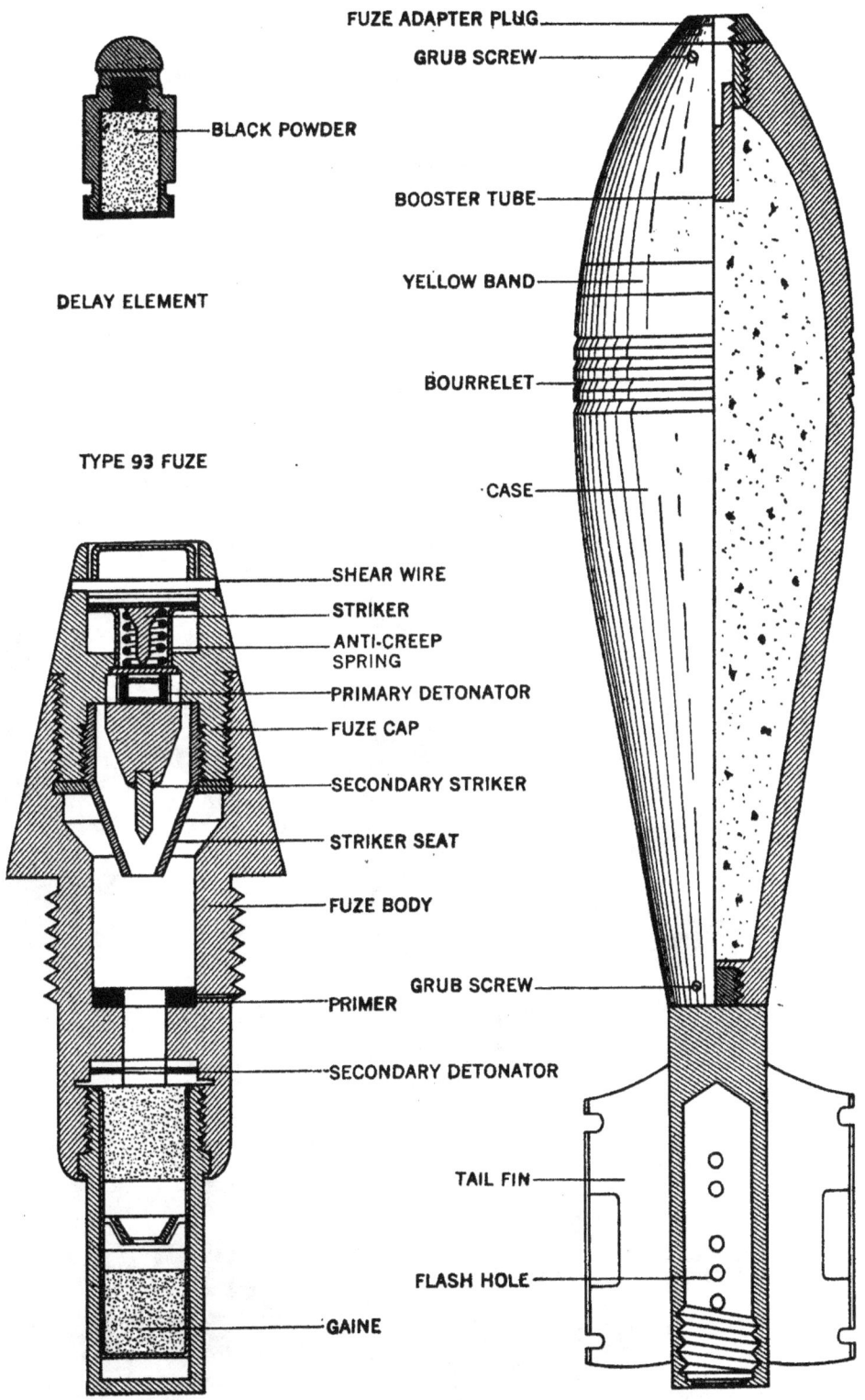

Figure 45.—15-cm mortar shell and Model 93 (1933) fuze.

25-cm Artillery Mortar

A Japanese 25-cm artillery (spigot) mortar was captured in the Imphal campaign. It is different in design from any weapon used by other armies and shows virtually no trace of foreign influences in its construction or employment. An outstanding feature is the fact that the 32-cm projectile outweighs the projector. This conforms to current Japanese theory, that heavy long-range guns have been supplanted by the airplane, and the tendency henceforth will be to utilize the lightest possible ground weapons

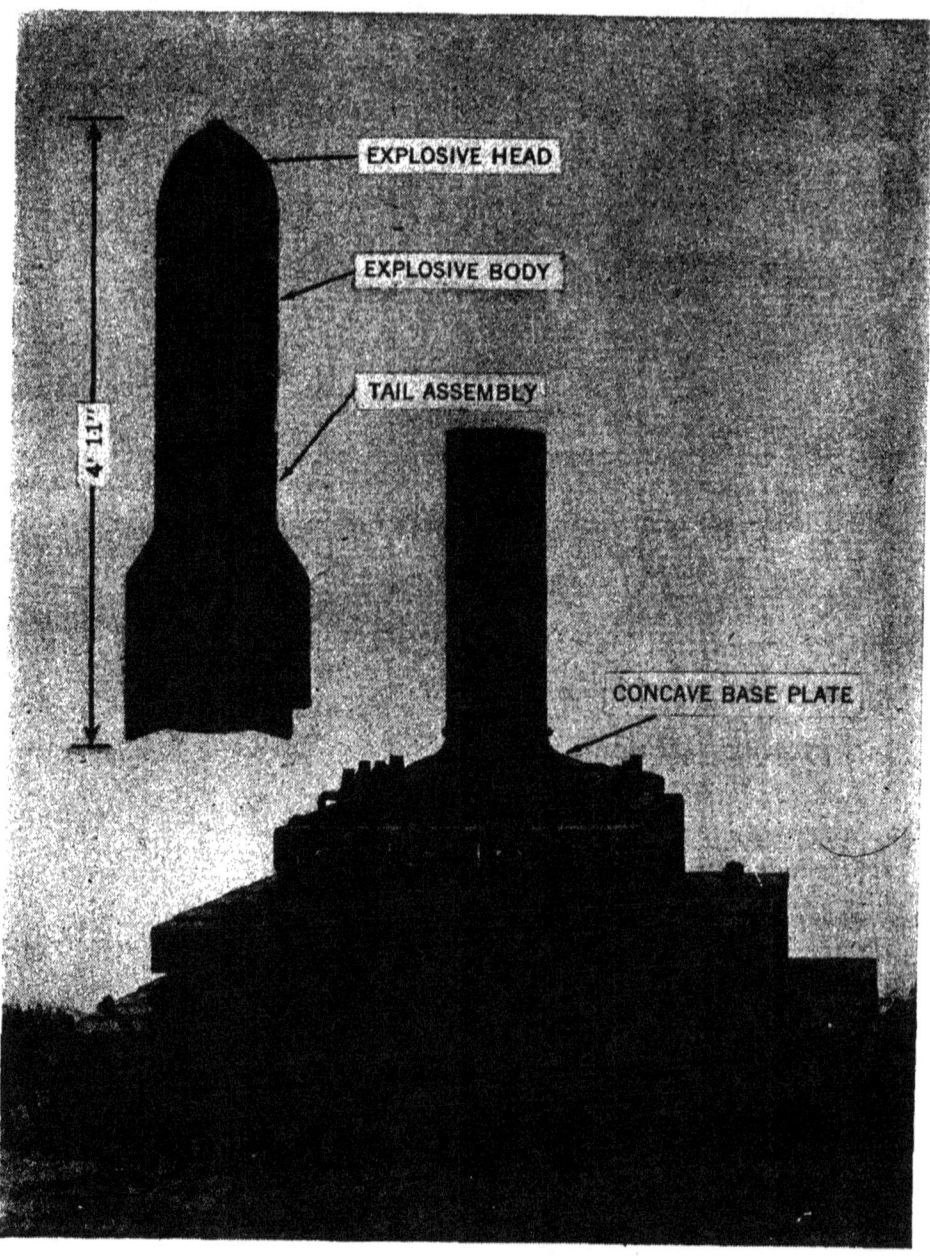

Figure 46.—25-cm artillery mortar (spigot) and shell.

which throw projectiles of the maximum practicable weight for short ranges. The complete mortar and projectile weigh about 2,000 pounds, and can be broken down into loads of 250 pounds or less, with the exception of the tail piece which weighs 350 pounds.

In order to project the large shell, the mortar itself is immobile. A total elevation of 150 mils is possible by changing the arrangement of the bolts which fix the mounting plate to the wooden base. Adjustments for range depend on variations in the amount of propellent increment. The weapon requires a large crew to service, and its rate of fire is very slow. Concussion allegedly is so great that the crew must remain in dugouts, or be at least about 500 yards away, when it fires. It also has been reported that only about 10 rounds can be fired after emplacement, since the weapon is thrown out of line by firing.

The mortar is a steel cylinder with a 256-mm bore. It is about 31 inches long and weighs 225 pounds. A cavity is machined in its top for the propellant. The tube is integral with a seating plate, which in turn seats on a mounting plate—a steel square, the central portion of which is slightly convex. This mounting plate rests on a larger square steel base, which in turn is supported by a wooden base, the three sections of which form a step-pyramid. When the desired line of fire is determined, the wooden base is emplaced in an excavation of about 1,000 cubic feet at an angle of 45 degrees.

The tube cavity for the propellant is machined downward from the muzzle. In the base of the cavity there is a threaded recess. When the propellent assembly is in position in this cavity, the recess takes the threaded end of the flash-train tube, centering it and locating the complete assembly. The tail assembly of the projectile is correctly positioned by plugs which engage slots in the tail.

There are four parts to the projectile assembly—the explosive head, the body, the tail, and the propellant. The head, which weighs 172 pounds, is 14.2 inches long and 12.48 inches in diameter. The body weighs 152 pounds and has an external length of 10.7 inches. The tail assembly, which has a total weight of 350 pounds, has four fins, each of which is supported by two wire struts. The external length of the whole assembly is 34.7 inches, and the diameter tapers from 12.48 inches at the top to 10.64 inches at the base.

Primary and increment charges of the propellant are contained within a brass case seated in the cavity of the spigot. A hollow metal tube, which contains the flash train, screws through a threaded orifice in the base of the case into the threaded recess of the spigot cavity. When in position, there are four flash holes at the base of the flash tube just below the primary charge. An igniter screws into the orifice in the side of the tail assembly of the projectile and is brought into close proximity to the ignition head of the flash tube. To fire, a safety washer is removed from the head of the initiating igniter which protrudes through the wall of the tail assembly.

Components of the propellent assembly, in addition to the brass case, are a 500-gram annular primary charge, a 400-gram annular increment, and four 100-gram circular increments. Then, there are one 50-gram increment in a large bag, and two 10-gram and four 5-gram increments in small bags, in addition to impact fuzes, one igniter, one friction pull igniter, and an electric igniter. Varying weights of the increments are necessary since range of the mortar is controlled entirely by graduations in the propellant.

☆ U. S. GOVERNMENT PRINTING OFFICE: 1945—629603

www.ingramcontent.com/pod-product-compliance
Lightning Source LLC
Chambersburg PA
CBHW080524110426
42742CB00017B/3229